SLEEPING
WITH A
STRANGER

SLEEPING WITH A STRANGER

How I Survived
Marriage to a Child Molester

Patricia Wiklund, Ph.D.

ADAMS PUBLISHING
Holbrook, Massachusetts

To J.D.

Copyright ©1995, Patricia Wiklund. All rights reserved. This book, or parts thereof, may not be reproduced in any form without permission from the publisher; exceptions are made for brief excerpts used in published reviews.

Published by Adams Media Corporation
260 Center Street, Holbrook, MA 02343

ISBN: 1-55850-443-5

Printed in the United States of America.

J I H G F E D C B A

Library of Congress Cataloging-in-Publication Data
Wiklund, Patricia.
Sleeping with a stranger : how I survived marriage to a child molester / Patricia Wiklund.
    p.   cm.
    Includes bibliographical references (p.   ) and index.
    ISBN 1-55850-443-5 (pbk.)
    1. Child molesters—United States—Family relationships. 2. Child molesters—United States—
Psychology. 3. Wiklund, Patricia. 4. Child molesters' spouses—United States—Biography. I. Title.
HV6570.2.W55   1995
364.1'536'092—dc20
[B]   95-7259
                                         CIP

This publication is designed to provide accurate and authoritative information with regard to the subject matter covered. It is sold with the understanding that the publisher is not engaged in rendering legal, accounting, or other professional advice. If legal advice or other expert assistance is required, the services of a competent professional person should be sought.
— From a *Declaration of Principles* jointly adopted by a Committee of the American Bar Association and a Committee of Publishers and Associations

This book is available at quantity discounts for bulk purchases.
For information, call 1-800-872-5627.

Cover design: Steve Snider

Table of Contents

Acknowledgments

While the initial experience was mine, this book could not have been written without the support of my family and friends. Their support while I cried and was going through the pain meant I could survive. Their support while I was healing challenged me to go on. Their support while I wrote the book meant the story could be told.

This book also could not have been written without the trust and courage of the many women who shared their stories with me. Whether anonymous strangers in chance meetings or clients who participated in ongoing treatment, my respect for them and my debt to them is considerable.

Introduction

What's a Nice Girl Like You...?

It is too great an audacity already now to draw a picture of the world, since there are still so many things which we cannot remotely anticipate.

— ALBERT EINSTEIN

Writing a book about a burning social issue that is also a burning personal issue gives rise to a variety of motivating factors. At first, I was just angry and I wanted to get revenge. I was angry at myself for getting into this situation, and for feeling so ineffective at getting out of it. But, the problem with using anger as the motivation for writing a book is that it doesn't have the staying power that writing a book demands. Anger is acting out and looking back, not pushing forward.

Then, I thought by writing this book people could begin to understand what had happened to me. Even people who knew me well, or who cared a lot about me, had a difficult time understanding what I experienced. Most people don't know, or can't see, the impact that being married to a child molester can have on your life. One close friend of mine could only say, "How difficult and sad it is for your ex-husband." She barely knew him, and yet her sympathy was for him, not me. I was deeply hurt that she could not understand or even see how difficult and sad it was for *me*. Over and over again people would deny my feelings and circumstances, saying that what I said was happening to me wasn't true, couldn't be happening. They didn't believe me. I had to have known, I had to be mistaken, I was wrong, they would say. My story wasn't true.

It was at this point that I started to think of myself as a hidden victim. But that was problematical too. I had strong needs for control, for being in charge. And I had strong needs for being seen as being in control. Seeing myself, or letting others see me, as a victim didn't feel good. Seeing myself as a victim implied I didn't, or couldn't, take charge of my own life. It defined my life as the woman who was married to a child molester. His inexorable behavior defined my life.

My own recovery was another motivating factor. This has been the most traumatic experience of my life. If I could get the story out, talk about it, hash it through, as writing a book would entail, I would be able to work through my hurt and anger, my sadness and grief. I was a "trained professional," but all my training neither prepared me for nor helped me deal with the pain I experienced. I felt so alone, like I was the only person who had ever gone through this experience. Writing it down would help diffuse the loneliness and pain.

Most importantly, now I see this as an opportunity to help others. When I was going through the experience, I found few supportive resources. Even my own therapist, while sympathetic, didn't seem sure of how to help me. Most therapists have not dealt with, or are willing to deal with, this issue. While an increasing amount of information is available on the topic and studies on victims of sexual abuse and their perpetrators are being published, there is still little, if anything, written that addresses the needs and issues of spouses or partners of child molesters.

When spouses or partners are mentioned in the professional literature, they are often portrayed as responsible for the perpetrator's sexual acting out. The spouse is seen as the cause of her husband's frustration, as the cause of his need to act out, or as colluding with his acting out as a way of avoiding her sexual responsibilities.

In victim literature the spouse of the molester is usually accused of colluding with the perpetrator. She is seen as neither protective enough to shield the child from the sexual advances of the perpetrator, nor aggressive enough to stop the abusive behavior.

"Mother's groups" focus on the relationship between the mother and the abused child. But seldom, if ever, are there support groups that focus on the woman as the spouse of the molester, and how she has been victimized by the consequences of her partner's abusive behavior. There is no place, and no sympathy, in the child abuse field for us.

While the primary purpose of this book is to shatter myths and dispense accurate, professional information, in the end, I suppose, my motivation for writing this book is probably a combination of all of the above. I also believe this is a story that demands to be written. At first, I didn't want to do it. I put my notes away for months on end and then would pull them out, flip through them, look at what I had written, write some more, and tuck away the file one more time. To say that I was, and am, ambivalent is an understatement. I think the book probably wrote itself, not just from my story but from the stories I have heard from other women in therapy groups, awareness groups, conferences for victims of sexual abuse, and sometimes, just in chance meetings.

There are still days when I get so angry, or when I feel so sad about the experience, that my desire for revenge, albeit unattractive, wells to the surface. On those days, I just want him to hurt as much as he has hurt other people. There is still a part of me that wants other people to understand and appreciate the hurt and anger I went through. I want to provide some solace to other women who are living through this. They are not alone. I want them to know there is someone else who has survived what they have experienced. There is someone else who understands. We are not alone.

Early on, in my own experience, when the pain and the anguish was still very new and I was still being very secretive, I happened to meet by chance another "hidden victim." I stopped one day for lunch at a deli in my neighborhood. With the combination of a busy lunchtime crowd and beautiful weather, I considered myself fortunate to find the last available table on the patio. I was just starting to eat my sandwich when a woman stopped and asked if she could share my table. Within moments, we were talking about the beautiful day, how nice it was to be outside, and how we both ended up at the same deli. I am not sure how the conversation shifted to where else we had been that day, but within moments we were talking about how we had both been to see our divorce lawyers that morning and how divorce was not "Plan A" when we were designing our lives.

As we talked about our marriages and the reasons we were leaving, we were both astounded to discover that both of our husbands had been sexually involved with children. The dam broke and we talked as if we had been lifelong best friends. As I finished lunch and was walking away from the table, I realized I never even asked her name, nor had I volunteered mine. But, her name wasn't important to me; my name wasn't important to her. What was important to both of us was that we had found someone else who was the spouse of a child molester. Someone who was uniquely qualified to understand our pain. Somehow it made all the difference, just knowing that I was not the only one. Someone else was not only going through the same situation, but understood what I was going through. Names didn't matter, but the shared experience made such an impact on me.

Stories of sexual molestation, unfortunately, are found in every neighborhood. The variety of statistics are alarming: approximately 20 percent of American families experience child sexual abuse. Of the 2 million cases of child abuse each year, about 300,000 are thought to involve sexual abuse, with the child in the most danger in his or her own home. One-third of the runaways in the United States come from families where sexual abuse has occurred. Two to four million cases of wife battering occur annually, and in 40 percent of the cases, child abuse also occurs. These are not just statistics and headlines, but stories of lives in quiet desperation.

Since the day of the chance meeting at the deli, I have talked to scores of women who have been a spouse or partner of a child molester. Everyone's story is its own version of hell. It is for these women that my story can no longer stay hidden. This book is for us.

Part I

Uncovering the Truth

Chapter 1

If It Can Happen to Me...

The trouble with the future is that it is no longer what it used to be.

— PAUL VALÉRY, French poet and philosopher

Sometimes it is hard to recognize beginnings. They have a tendency to happen so subtly, without telling of the events to follow. Then looking back, the circumstances you remember about that marker event seem very strange.

For me, the beginning of the end came in March 1983. From outward appearances we were the perfect couple. Well educated at good schools, we started our own business that was running successfully for a number of years. Married for fifteen years, we were raising a beautiful ten-year-old son who was the apple of my eye, were living in a house that we had fixed up ourselves, had many friends and family living close by.

Both of our careers were in transition. After fulfilling his childhood dream to develop a school and residential treatment facility for emotionally troubled teens, my husband drifted without a career focus in his life. He worked with several child care agencies, especially one residential treatment center for troubled boys. In addition, he saw clients in the offices we shared with several other therapists. But he was missing the passion and drive he had when he was working on his dream project.

After years as a therapist and college professor, I finished my Ph.D. and now was searching for another challenge. I was increasingly successful as a professional speaker and seminar leader. This meant a shift from the entry-level, mostly free or low-fee speaking engagements to big-time corporate work.

As I was becoming more successful, he was drifting. I was busy making more money and getting more recognition. We were both struggling with the impact of these changes.

I had been working in another city, about one hundred miles away, for a few days, and I remembered thinking as I drove home that I was skilled and talented enough to make it "big time" in my business. I had tested myself against a major Fortune 100 company audience and had done great. It was late when I got home, so my conversation with my husband was short, mostly checking logistics, and then I fell into bed.

The next morning I was still sleeping when the phone rang. I vaguely remembered my husband leaving early for a meeting downtown, and it finally dawned on me that I had to answer the phone.

It was my husband, crying, on the other end of the line. Panic and terror spilled out with every confused word. He had been arrested for child molestation and he was in jail. He asked me to call our friend, Steve, who was a criminal attorney. My first reaction was to take charge and to take care of him. I told him to stop crying, and to pull himself together. It must be a mistake, it would be straightened out soon.

As I went through that day, I was surprised by the reactions of his colleagues, employers, and friends. They wouldn't talk to me, they removed him from his job, and they wouldn't give me any information about what was going on, or what they knew. For someone like myself who has a great need for control, it was very difficult. I still had the fantasy that I could fix things for him.

Based on the belief of his innocence, my reaction to his being arrested was to hold my head up high, act the part of the wronged victim, and go forth with my banner and cause. When he said he wouldn't go to church that Sunday, I insisted, and pointed out that if we didn't go, as we did every other Sunday, people would think for sure that he was guilty.

When houseguests came the next week, I honored his request not to tell them what had happened. I kept the secret. I was as ashamed as he seemed to be. Even though I had worked with clients who had sexual problems, I never imagined that anyone I knew or loved would be so bedeviled. I had certainly not expected to be married to someone who was arrested for something so awful. People like me just didn't have this problem.

Formal charges were never brought against him. Apparently the police had jumped the gun, arresting him before the grand jury had brought in an indictment. The case was left open, meaning it could be activated if any new allegations came to light.

Looking back, I realize now that the biggest mistake I made that day was to believe him when he lied to me. He had told me when he called from jail that he was innocent. He said the charges came from kids who were picking on him, who were lying. I didn't even think about asking him if the charges were true. I just assumed they were false. It became a familiar theme, his reassuring me that things were okay, when in fact they weren't, and that he had actually done what people had accused him of.

Underneath my bravado and stoic face, though, I recognized that our marriage wasn't all so wonderful, and hadn't been for some time. Troubles were building. We were frustrated with infertility, and I blamed our increasing lack of sexual relations on the pressures and the hassles of having to time our lovemaking with thermometers and calendars.

Money was also an issue between us. We found it hard to save and invest. We lived from paycheck to paycheck, and since being self-employed, the paychecks weren't all that regular. We made good money, but we could sure spend it, too.

We were spending more time working or with friends than each other. It was almost as if we were roommates, not mates. We had drifted apart. I assumed the professional issues were the root of the relationship issues that we were experiencing.

There had been one incident the previous fall that could have been a portent of things to come. But I dismissed it as the ranting of a crazy lady.

We had once taken in as a foster child a teenager who had been my husband's client. The boy had been a resident at one of the programs for emotionally disturbed teens. The placement in our home lasted only a short time because it became evident that the young man was getting worse, not better. He was having behavior problems, lying, and becoming more withdrawn. I feared he would put all of us in danger. One day I came into his bedroom to find his bed on fire. He was staring at a drop of water on the side of his drinking glass, oblivious to the flames. I called the state hospital to arrange his admission. The caseworker, my husband, and the boy all wanted to continue his placement with us. However, I had reached my limit. I insisted he be hospitalized. I wanted nothing more to do with him. My husband visited him in the hospital, but we never talked about him again.

When the boy was finally discharged from the hospital, he drifted off to California. I didn't give him much more thought after that, at least not until the fall of 1982, some eight years after he had lived with us. Late one afternoon, a disheveled woman came bursting through my office door, demanding to speak with me. I led her into the consulting room, and was hit with a barrage of accusations, pleas for help, and general hysterics. She said she had proof that her husband (the adolescent we took in) had been seduced and sexually molested by my husband while in therapy with him, during residential treatment, and while living at our house. She said that my husband and the young man had kept in close contact after that time.

She had been one of the caseworkers he was assigned to when living in California. A personal relationship had developed between them, and, although he was almost twenty years younger than she, she said they fell in love and married. The boy left her, returned to town, and was making a living by prostituting himself. She claimed it was my responsibility to find him, and to rescue him from this terrible situation, because, after all, it was my husband who started him down this path. I tried to calm her down, to explain it was not my responsibility to find her husband. Whatever issues she had with her husband were part of their relationship, and it wasn't my job to fix things. In the midst of the conversation, she jumped up, told me I'd be sorry for not helping her, and she would get my husband for abusing her husband.

As much as I didn't believe her ranting, her visit shook me up. It broke through my defenses and started a nagging feeling that something might be very wrong. I knew what my husband would say if I mentioned the incident to him. He had become more and more convinced that former clients and colleagues were picking on him, trying to make trouble for him. This would be one more incident to prove there were people out to get him. I talked to a trusted friend and advisor, and to one of our priests. I asked myself if I wanted to be in this marriage. What if her allegations were true? Even if they weren't true, how much trouble could a crazy kid cause? Would I be caught up in his difficulties?

As a part of my professional training I had been in therapy for a number of years. We were required to check in with an experienced therapist on a regular basis as we learned how to be therapists. I learned a lot about myself, how I had been affected by my family, by my early life experiences, and by the choices I made for myself. The therapy was especially helpful to me with what I called my neurosis of choice: depression. For as long as I could remember, I experienced a low-level, chronic depression, a shadow on my life. Now it was lifting, and, for the most part, I experienced many days of joy and satisfaction. There were fewer days where my chest felt heavy, as if someone or something was sitting on it, fewer days of wanting to withdraw and just be by myself.

But now this crazy lady and her accusations brought up new concerns. Was my marriage contributing to my depression? What if he had done what she described? What if, what if, what if . . . . I was forced to look more closely at my life. Finally I knew I had to do something to make things change. So I told my husband I wanted a separation.

His response was to promise me anything, including going into therapy, getting some help so I wouldn't leave. I wanted him to figure out what he wanted in his life so that we could continue our life together. Unlike my training, his professional training had not included personal therapy. The motto in his training program was, "We don't get therapy, we give therapy." For years he had resisted looking at any issues he might have. For years he had avoided therapy. Now he was desperate to do anything so that we could stay together.

He did go. He worked alone, and we worked together through the fall and winter. The more I participated, the more I came to believe therapy was not working for him. He was plagued by demons I didn't know about and couldn't address.

I had already decided I would leave my marriage when the call from the jail came. Then I was stuck. How could I separate from a man who had just been accused of such heinous crimes? I stayed with him so that people would not think that he was guilty. My presence by his side would testify to his innocence. I wanted to believe he was innocent. I didn't even want to think he was guilty. I didn't want my life to crumble.

Life settled into an unreal dailiness. I got up in the morning, went to work, and avoided dealing with the feelings I was having. By June, it became evident that our problems were getting worse rather than better, and that I was getting more and more depressed. I knew our marriage was over and my staying would not revive it, or help my husband with his personal struggles. I finally moved into an apartment not far from the house we shared.

The criminal attorney we hired said that there would be a hundred days of hell following my husband's arrest. The hundred days became a thousand, and then more.

The next year could be aptly called the year of the living dead. Money was very tight. The agencies my husband worked with suspended his contracts until the charges could be resolved. He spent most of his time on various legal issues; it was difficult for him to work.

Under the pressure of our diminished income, we filed for bankruptcy. I was numb as I sat in court watching our life come crashing down. Driving home, my throat was scratchy. By the time I got home, I had the sniffles. I flopped on my bed, and woke up three hours later with a miserable cold. I gave up the struggle and succumbed to the depression that had been hanging around the edges for months. I took to my bed and got up six weeks later. The combination of stress and depression did me in.

I coasted for the next several months, struggling with depression, knowing that I was going to get a divorce. But the time never seemed right to get it started. Besides, starting legal proceedings meant hiring another attorney and dredging up all the pain and frustration of having to deal with things. It seemed easier to just let things slide. I developed the pattern of just getting through the day. I was still living in the apartment close to our house, and we could share custody of our son. Logistically it all made sense.

If the beginning of the end came in March 1983, the end came in late spring 1984. I heard that a former neighbor had moved back into town and, on a whim one day, I picked up the phone and called her for lunch. We had lots to catch up on: her kids, my kid, her life, my life. We had lived next door to one another for almost ten years, but hadn't seen each other for over two years.

During lunch we talked and talked. If she asked once, she asked a dozen times. Was I really going to get a divorce? I kept saying yes, but . . . the time isn't right, it seems like a pain, things weren't so bad the way they were. I always said yes to her question, but then gave her many reasons why the time was just not right. We were well into the second hour of our lunch when she finally said she had something to tell me. She was so serious, not at all the upbeat and optimistic friend I had known and loved.

And then the ax fell. She was sure the charges against him were true . . . her son was one of the children he molested.

This was a child I had diapered. I had wiped his tears and runny nose. His shy smile was as precious to me as that of my own son. This family was not just a neighbor, but our dear friends. They had been there for us, as we had been there for them. We had cried together over family tragedies and had celebrated the births of our children together. For years we had been an extended family as young families in suburbs often are. To have him damage this child was, and is, a pain that is excruciating.

If the first shoe had dropped the day he was arrested, the other shoe dropped at lunch that day. The enormity of it all was too much to process. All I wanted was out—to get my child and myself out of the marriage, out of town, and out of the situation. I was hurt, angry, and ashamed. I wanted him dead.

I had visions of a Mack truck crushing him on the freeway. The upside of an accident was that it would get him out of my life and the double indemnity clause on his life insurance. He was worth a quarter of a million dollars dead. Alive, there was just the promise of pain—financial and emotional. Then I decided none of this quick snuff-out stuff was enough. I wanted him to suffer, to hurt like his victims were hurting, like how I was hurting. Scenes of torture dredged up from old novels and slasher movies came to my mind. Nothing was too cruel for him.

I couldn't believe I was feeling this way, that I was thinking what I was thinking. This was not me. I am not a violent, malicious, or vengeful person. The depth of my rage startled me. I did not believe I was capable of such feelings. Little was I to know they were just the beginning.

I know I drove home that day, but I have no conscious memories of it. Like accident victims who can't remember the impact, there is a time in my life that is gone. Looking back, I am sure I was in shock. My belief in his innocence, my belief in his reassurances that the charges simply involved crazy kids trying to hurt him, my naive belief that my life would somehow get back to what I wanted it to be, was shattered. There was no question my neighbor was telling the truth. There was no question her son had been truthful when he had told his mother about the molestation, at our cabin in the woods, with our son in the next room asleep. There was no question. It had happened.

Later that week, when I was talking to my attorney, I got a glimpse of the long road ahead. When I told her that one of the issues of the divorce would be my husband's molesting of his patients, neighborhood children, and our son's friends, she told me that everyone makes those accusations and that it isn't smart to use that strategy to muddy the waters of the divorce. She couldn't believe that in this case it was true. It was the first time I came up against professionals not supporting or believing what I was convinced was true. It would not be the last time. When I gave her the evidence, she quickly became supportive, not only of this issue, but also of me professionally when issues of our practice and my culpability were raised by ongoing investigations and suits.

If the previous year had been living hell, this was worse. He was denying everything, our son was being pitted against one or the other of us, I was angry, frightened, and on a roller coaster of emotions. How could my life have ended up in this mess?

The only thing that kept me going was work. I saw clients, delivered presentations, worked on professional committees, traveled, and compartmentalized my life. My personal issues and difficulties did not exist while I was working.

I worked hard at keeping secrets. I told few people what was actually happening. I didn't even tell my parents. I didn't want anyone to know. The shame was too great. I felt responsible, not only for what he had done, but also for fixing things, for making this incredible wrong somehow right. I remember thinking there was some secret, some magic escape. I just had to find it. And, of course, no matter how hard I tried, no matter where I looked, I just couldn't find it. The secret was, there was no secret. No magic could restore my life to its former state. I couldn't go back.

Eventually, the divorce was final. He insisted to the very end that he was innocent. He felt he hadn't done anything wrong, even when his victims gave sworn, taped statements. He only backed off of demands for sole custody of our son when I threatened to go to a full jury trial, with the videos of his victims as my witnesses.

Shortly after the divorce, I moved with my son across the country to a community near my major consulting client. The charges that had not come up during the divorce were threatening to surface as the investigation by the state board of professional examiners heated up. I wanted my son out of town before the story became front-page news.

The civil cases went on and on. Children he had abused filed suits for damages and malpractice. Living in a community property state, and having been in business together, I found myself being named as a defendant in these cases, and held liable for damages as a consequence of his behavior. I was being interviewed by caseworkers and attorneys for all sides, named in a malpractice case as a defendant, and then assigned the same attorney as my husband. At one point, I was called as a witness for the plaintiff while I was the defendant. I testified for eight hours one day, being asked questions in turn by eight to ten attorneys.

The legal issues were expensive, demeaning, and distracting. I hadn't done anything, and yet kept being named in the suits. When I complained to my attorney that it wasn't fair, she explained that since he had abused clients and I had benefited from his income, I was liable. It was a nightmare.

At one deposition, I learned there had been an ongoing investigation of allegations that stretched back over ten years. When I confronted the sex crimes officers on why I had never been informed, they told me it was standard procedure. They keep the wife in the dark about the investigation because "she always sides with her husband and helps him cover up."

Friends and family members came forward with incidents they had witnessed, incidents that seemed innocent at the time, but in retrospect were corroborating evidence of his wrongdoing. When I asked them why no one had said anything, they answered they didn't realize what was going on, or if they did, they didn't want to upset me.

Eventually the civil cases were settled, and the plaintiffs received cash awards funded by the malpractice insurance. The criminal case was left open. It was never brought to trial. The prosecutors didn't feel the victims would make credible witnesses.

I kept looking for a way to control what was going on. I felt I was at the mercy of the courts and of attorneys representing other people's interests. There was nothing that I could do. I felt like I was at the beach, standing in the waves and being knocked down. Every time I tried to stand up, another wave would come and knock me down again. I was looking for a secret, a way I could stand up, a way to take control of my life. What I discovered is, there is no secret, there is no magic formula, and it would be a long time before I would be able to take charge of a situation I could not control and get my life back in order.

I can remember the day, but not the date. I know it was November, because it was cold outside. My bedroom was warm from the late morning sun coming in the window. I was sitting on my bed half-dressed. I had just gotten off the phone, trying to arrange a holiday visit for my son with his father. And then I got it.

I finally understood that my ex-husband wasn't going to change, that he wasn't going to be any different from what he had been. He was a child molester. And I remember saying to myself . . . there he is, satisfied and smug, denying he did anything wrong. He is still not taking any responsibility for what he did, for what happened. He wasn't feeling any guilt, or any pain. He was doing just fine. And there I sat, in agony over what he did, miserable, blaming myself, and trying to figure out how to change what already happened. I was letting him ruin my life. He wasn't ruining his life, but I was letting him ruin mine. I was too focused on feeling guilty because I had not seen what was happening. But, he was the guilty one. He, not I, had brought this great injustice into my life.

It was a moment of truth, an epiphany, a revelation of what I had let him do, an empowering realization, that although I couldn't control what had happened, I could certainly take charge of what I was going to do about it.

I grabbed a piece of paper, titled it "Pat's Treatment Plan," and got to work. I had been a therapist for years. I had developed and implemented countless treatment plans for other people, and they got better. Now it was my time. I wanted, and needed, to take care of myself like I had taken care of others. I remember sitting in the sun, with sheets of paper flying, laughing to myself. I knew what I was doing, I knew what I needed to do, and I would do it. I would no longer let that idiot ruin my life. I was worth more than that.

It took awhile. It wasn't easy. I found a therapist that was both supportive and confrontive. I signed up for several seminars and conferences on child abuse and pedophilia. I read everything I could get my hands on. I took three intensive week-long self-awareness training sessions. I got a cat, and then a dog. I had my makeup done, bought new clothes, and got my hair permed. I bought myself some jewelry. I joined a support group. I covered all my bases. And it took time. Longer than I would have thought. But looking back, I hadn't realized how much work there was to do.

But there is a path through this experience and I have learned that there is life again on the other side. It is a long, difficult process, but it is worth the struggle. My only hope is that I can provide insight and encouragement to others, and that we might all learn from my experiences.

I am one victim who refuses to hide any more.

Chapter 2

Inside the Mind of a Child Molester

Offenders don't have horns and a tail. They look like nice guys. They are not strangers. Everyone tells you to say no to strangers. No one tells you to say no to your family.

— INCEST SURVIVOR

Professionals, family members, and victims have struggled to understand why child molesters do what they do. A variety of theories have been proposed in an attempt to develop treatment programs, to deal with the pain and anguish of being victimized, or to determine causal behaviors. There is no consensus on what makes up a child molester. There are a variety of conflicting views and, in fact, we may not know or understand why some people act this way. What we do know is what child molesters and pedophiles do.

It is tempting to believe that the pattern of behavior that one molester follows is the only way, or the primary way that all molesters behave. This is not always true. The Federal Bureau of Investigation (FBI), in their Behavioral Science Unit, has reviewed the patterns of abuse and the public's response to this abuse in an effort to make sense of this epidemic. If we understand more about what molesters do, we can start to deal more effectively with why they do what they do and the impact their behavior has on others.

The FBI makes clear distinction between actions—what people do—and thoughts—what people think about doing. From the criminal perspective, a person must have molested a child to be charged with the crime. Thinking about it, fantasizing about it, talking to others about what they want to do, are not against the law, and therefore are not instances of molesting.

This is a different viewpoint from the psychological perspective, that upholds the essential feature for diagnosing pedophilia is the recurrent, intense sexual urges and sexually arousing fantasies involving sexual activity with a prepubescent child. These urges may either be acted upon, or be sufficiently disturbing to the individual that they are markedly distressed by them. The key factor for a diagnosis of pedophilia is being sexually attracted to children. The key factor in being labeled a child molester is sexually acting out with children. It is interesting to note that many people who molest children are not pedophiles; that is, their primary sexual attraction is not to children, even though they have been sexual with children.

"STRANGER DANGER"

The FBI incidence patterns have defused the emphasis on "stranger danger" as the primary pattern of child molesting. Historically, parents and teachers have told children to beware of strangers, not to accept rides, not to take candies or favors from strangers, to "say no, yell, and tell" when approached by a stranger. The stereotype molester has been the shady character in a trench coat hanging around school playgrounds. The FBI found that this category of child molester has the least incidence. The lurid tales in the media notwithstanding, children are much more in danger in their own families or from trusted acquaintances than from the stranger on the street.

TWO TYPES OF MOLESTERS

The FBI describes two types of child molesters: the situational molester and the preferential molester. The situational molester is not necessarily a pedophile; that is, he *is not* primarily sexually attracted to children. The preferential molester *is* primarily sexually attracted to children. There are important differences in how these two types of molesters are sexually involved with children.[1]

Situational Molesters

Situational molesters are more common, but have fewer victims. The FBI estimates that a typical situational molester averages eighty-one incidents of molesting, with an average of two victims each. Situational molesters are overrepresented by lower socioeconomic groups. They are not primarily sexually attracted to children, but do have sex with children for a variety of reasons. Four patterns of situational molesting have been identified:

REPRESSED: This man usually has low self-esteem and poor coping skills. He turns to children as a substitute for his preferred partners. He will often abuse his own children, or coerce a child into compliance.

MORALLY INDISCRIMINATE: Sexual abuse is only a part of the general pattern of abuse for this molester. He will use and abuse anyone, any way he can. Often the victim is the weakest or most vulnerable person around. He will abuse his own kids, strangers, and acquaintances. He seems to lack a conscience.

SEXUALLY INDISCRIMINATE: The motto for this person is "If it feels good, do it." He will try any and all sexual behaviors, seemingly out of boredom.

INADEQUATE: This fellow hangs around school yards. He is a social misfit, withdrawn, unusual, eccentric. He sees children as non-threatening sexual partners. He may have mental or emotional problems.

---

[1] Throughout this book, I've referred to molesters by the male gender for the purposes of clarity and consistency. While it is not always the case that the molester is male, it does reflect the norm. FBI statistics show that as many as 90 percent of molesters are men.

Preferential Molesters

Preferential molesters are the primary sexual exploiters of children. Their income and occupations are typically higher than situational molesters and include professionals such as physicians, police officers, child welfare workers, ministers, and child therapists. They also include people who work informally with children such as camp counselors and baby-sitters. Their sexual preference is for children and they act on their preferences in highly predictable and repetitive ways. They develop sexual rituals and stylized patterns of behavior, and persist in acting them out, even when their behavior may be self-destructive. Preferential molesters average 282 incidents of molesting with an average of 150 victims each.

Preferential child molesters are the most dangerous molesters because they are the most skilled, devious, and committed. They gain access to a child by first being a friend, relative, or family friend. In some cases the parents are seduced with friendship to gain access to the child. The victim/molester bond may be extremely tight, with most of the victims never disclosing the abuse. Once targeted, a child has little chance of escaping the molester.

Three patterns of preferential molesters have been identified:

SEDUCERS: This molester seduces children by actively courting them over a period of time. Many of these molesters have multiple victims at any one time, sometimes classmates, teammates, or children from the same neighborhood. Ensuring the children will "keep the secret" is a primary issue, especially as the molester stops seeing a child who has grown beyond his age preference.

INTROVERTED: These molesters are very similar to the inadequate situational molester but are primarily sexually attracted to children. They lack the interpersonal skills to relate to children, so they target the youngest, most vulnerable child, hang out where children are likely to gather, and may limit acting out to just watching children while masturbating or exposing themselves to children without touching or talking to them.

SADISTIC: Sadistic molesters are not only primarily sexually attracted to children, but want to inflict psychological or physical pain on their victims. These are the stereotype child molesters who abduct children from the street or shopping malls, molest them, and kill them. Although these molesters get a lot of media coverage and are the focus of both parental and children's fears, they are the *least common* type of molesters, having the fewest victims.

Ross Nelson is typical of a seductive preferential molester. He described his seduction routine and targeting in an April 1992 *Redbook* magazine article. For more than forty years he had sex with boys, convincing himself that his time with the boy had a more positive influence on the child than a negative one. Ross claimed he never had to force or intimidate the children, offer them money, or offer them bribes to come with him. The boys, he said, came willingly. Nelson stalked young boys in shopping malls with a well-planned pattern of advances and retreats designed to convince the child that there was nothing to fear from this friendly man.

Nelson worked for awhile in a photo finishing lab where the amount of pornography involving children helped convince him that his desires were not abnormal. He goes on to conclude:

> *I have been judged and found guilty, yet I've never really thought what I was doing was wrong. What did I take from a boy? His innocence? His childhood? I don't think so. I made advances, yes, but I never forced myself on a boy. He is not deaf, dumb, and blind; he is aware of innuendo, dirty jokes, overt sexuality. Parents have themselves to blame if their sons haven't learned the values and morals they need to say no to a man like me.*

Nelson refused to participate in treatment while in prison because the intent of the treatment was to instill in the molesters a fear of children. He shows no remorse for what he has done. He also accepts no responsibility, denying that what he did was even harmful to the children. He blames the children for not resisting what can only be described as stalking. He blames the parents for not being the kind of parents they should. He even blames his arrest and prosecution on the coerced statements of two of his victims. In no way does he blame himself for anything. This is not the pattern of a man caught up in the heat of the moment, but rather a well-planned and executed pattern of abuse and victimization.

Preferential child molesters typically share four characteristics:

1. They have a long-term pattern of problematic sexual experience. Many molesters have had a sexualized childhood. They may have a history of sexual abuse, sexual acting out, or sexual withdrawal. Often they are seen as "troubled teens" or have "troubles" in their military service without the trouble being defined or labeled.

2. They often never marry, live alone or with their parents, and have limited dating experience. If they do marry, they choose either strong and domineering or weak and passive women. In their marriages they usually demonstrate a low sex drive. They may marry for cover or to gain access to a woman's children. They do not socialize or easily form adult social relationships.

3. They are skilled at seduction techniques. Preferential molesters are skilled at targeting victims, and can pick out of a group of children the one who is needy, emotional or physically neglected, or from a broken home. They are like pied pipers, attracting children to them. They prefer a specific age and gender. How old the child looks and acts is more important to them than the chronological age of the child. They have access to children—in their neighborhood, at their jobs, through their volunteer activities, through their hobbies, or by hiring children to work for them. They seduce children with gifts, affection, and attention, and by targeting and courting the children. They manipulate children with sexuality, often by sharing pornography with them.

4. They have sexual fantasies of children. They have excessive interest in and association with children. They hang out with kids, have children as friends. They may have youthful decor in their house, including toys and games. They often will collect child pornography or photograph children themselves.

Situational molesters and preferential molesters differ in a number of ways. For a situational molester, sexually acting out with children accompanies others forms of abuse or is opportunistic. For preferential molesters, sexual relations with children is their primary objective. The likelihood of changing or "curing" situational molesters depends on dealing with their whole pattern of abusive behavior, and is very difficult. For all practical purposes, the likelihood of changing or "curing" preferential molesters is impossible. Like Nelson, they see little wrong in what they do, and little need for change.

IN THEIR OWN DEFENSE

Nelson follows the pattern of most child molesters because he disclaims any responsibility for what he did and denies that what he did was harmful, or his fault. The FBI found that all molesters have a variety of excuses and defenses for their behavior when they are caught. They attempt to deny, minimize, excuse, or justify their behavior.

Strong denial is usually the first reaction, not just by the molester but also by his friends, family, and colleagues. In the case of situational molesters, this denial may be the initial reaction we all have to difficult or uncomfortable events: the initial, "Oh, no, it couldn't be." This response may be better characterized by the phrase "I don't want it to be true" rather than it isn't true. This is especially the case with family and friends. We don't want to have to admit what happened. Situational molesters deny their actions as long as possible, turning the tables and suggesting the accuser is lying, the children seduced them, or they can't remember what happened because they were drunk or high. The denial of preferential molesters may be more devious. It is not unusual for them to continue to deny what they have done for a long time. They may also claim that they are the innocent victims, that terrible people are out to destroy them.

If a molester can no longer deny his actions in the face of mounting evidence, he may attempt to minimize the types of activity, lie about the number of incidents, or characterize his action as nonsexual affection. (It is also not uncommon for victims to deny or minimize their contact with their molesters. A child, or more likely a teen, may not admit what has been happening out of his or her own fear or shame, even when confronted by photos or eyewitness testimony.)

Preferential molesters are very clever in coming up with good reasons to justify their contact with kids. They may fall back on their professional responsibilities to fabricate a context that would justify their behavior. It's not uncommon to hear about the minister who took the youth group on a spiritual retreat and then developed the theme of temptations of the flesh. The child psychologist who claimed the "hugging" was just good therapy. The police officer who was investigating child prostitution or child pornography. These "good reasons" as an excuse for inappropriate behavior cover the reality of a molester meeting his own needs. Minimizing, denying, and/or excusing a molester's behavior as misunderstood or misinterpreted allows the molester to avoid taking responsibility for what he did. It places the responsibility on the child, or on the parents for not raising the child with strong enough moral values. It allows the molester to see himself as the victim rather than the perpetrator.

Mental illness, and more recently addiction, is also used to explain why molesters exhibit the behavior they do. While some molesters will feign mental illness, others will come upon the defense when all else has failed. There is a difference between mental illness as a clinical diagnosis and as a condition that meets the legal judgment of diminished responsibility and competency.

In a 1994 Maryland case, a man who was charged with eighty-four counts of child abuse and child pornography entered a plea of insanity because he had irresistible urges to sexually abuse children. The court was charged with deciding if he was unable to obey the law as the result of a mental disease or mental defect. The defendant was described as a man who preyed on youths from poorer families, by luring them to his home with gifts and all-day outings. He would then molest them and have an accomplice record the sexual acts on videotape. When he was arrested, he had an extensive collection of pornography with young children, including over 3,200 videotapes. He exhibited a pattern of behavior typical of a preferential molester. Yet, he claimed he was mentally ill. The court did not allow his plea of insanity, and held him accountable for his behavior.

A more lethal defense is a request to "overlook" the molestation because of the contributions that the molester may have made in other areas. This is a particularly potent defense if the man is a leader in the community or holds a position of importance in the community or business. It is as if we agree to overlook this "one little flaw" in light of his larger contributions.

Sometimes molesters will plea bargain, or make settlements with their victims, either out of "concern for the privacy and feelings of the victim" or to minimize the disruption to the family or their own lives. The rationale is that it is cheaper or less bothersome to settle on a cash award than to go through a lengthy, expensive trial. The molester then gets to plead guilty without admitting to being guilty and serving the appropriate criminal sentence.

WHY DO THEY DO THIS?

The behavior patterns of child molesters, both situational and preferential, describe what they do. But, these descriptions aren't enough for most people.

We also want to know *why* they do what they do. We want to understand what made them do it. Sometimes we want to know who can be blamed, or how to stop them from doing it again, or even how to prevent others from getting into the same situations.

One of the most common explanations for why someone becomes a molester is that he was abused as a child himself. And when we look at the demographics and statistics, there are a variety of studies that have reported anywhere from 30 to 75 percent of all adults who molest children were, in fact, molested themselves when they were children. It would be tempting to excuse their behavior, or at least explain it by saying they were so traumatized as children, it's understandable that they're acting out in this way.

But just because this explanation is common doesn't necessarily make it true. It is a theory, or a best guess as to why things happen. Experts need to be very careful in going from a general theory to why a specific instance occurred. The theory gives professionals a starting point to begin understanding the makeup of a molester. But victims and professionals alike can get into trouble if they assume a theory is always the truth and reality, rather than just an attempt to make sense out of their experiences.

The role of theory in understanding the relationship of childhood experience and later adult behavior is especially tricky. Most of us want a theory that clearly predicts specific adult behaviors that result from specific childhood experiences. Unfortunately, this is seldom the case. Although we want a direct route from childhood to adulthood, the route is almost always twisted, uncertain, and subject to a variety of external and internal issues. There are issues that must be understood if we want to understand the reasons some people molest children. We need to understand the difference between necessary and sufficient, between correlation and causation, and why being a victim does not excuse a person from victimizing others.

Necessary But Not Sufficient

The first issue is what has sometimes been called "necessary but not sufficient." This simply means that while a previous condition may have been *necessary* for a later event to occur, there's no guarantee that the later event will occur, nor is there any *sufficient* evidence that this is the only previous action that can lead to these consequences.

For example, I love to garden. In the springtime when the ground gets soft and starts to get warm from the spring rains, you'll find me planting seeds in my garden. Planting a seed is necessary for a flower, a bush, or a tree to sprout. However, as necessary as it is, it's not sufficient, it's not enough. I also have to make sure the seed is watered, is covered properly, is fertilized adequately, and the type of soil is appropriate for the type of plant that I'm growing. I even need to insure the overall environment and climatic conditions of my garden are appropriate to the seed I planted. If I plant zinnias in a shady, moist area, it is unlikely many plants will grow, and those that do grow will be stunted with fewer flowers than if I had planted them in a sunny corner of an open flower bed. It also wouldn't do to plant an orange tree in that same sunny corner of the flower bed. The seed may sprout, but living where I do on the East Coast, no matter how sunny the summer, the orange tree would not survive outside in our winter weather.

Sometimes I get a surprise in my garden. A plant will sprout and grow, even flower, without my having planted a seed. In gardening circles these are called volunteers. Sometimes they are the result of plants putting out seeds without your being aware of it. One year it was lily of the valley, another year some weird-looking marigolds. Both lasted one year and never came back. I never knew where they came from.

So, what do orange trees and volunteer marigolds have to do with child molesters? Many, but not all, child molesters report being molested as children. Some therapists and theorists suggest that being molested as a child can start an individual on the path of being a child molester. However, the path is not so certain. While being molested as a child may be one of the antecedent causes of being a child molester, there is a large number of people who have been molested themselves who never molest children. There are also some people who were never molested as children who turn out to be child molesters as adults. So, while an early pattern of abuse may be a contributing factor, there are certainly other mitigating factors that can influence a person as well.

Correlation and Causation

The other concept that is necessary to address when looking at early childhood experience and later adult behavior is the concept of causation and correlation. It is common to look at two events that happen at the same time (being correlated with one another) and then make the assumption that the one event causes the other. In fact they may be completely unconnected.

Let's go back to my garden. I order seeds by mail, usually relying on two favorite companies I have used for years. But, I also often try new or exotic varieties from new companies. One year I planted my "exotics" in a specially prepared bed, rich in horse manure. I gave my expensive new seedlings the best of everything, only to see them all die off while my old favorites from the tried and true suppliers thrived.

It would be easy to attribute the cause of seedling failure to the poor seeds this unfamiliar supplier had sent me. After all, only that company's seeds failed. The other two companies' seeds thrived. But on further research, the failure was only correlated with their company of origin. The true cause was the load of horse manure. I had inadvertently loaded up with the current year's manure crop, rather than with composted manure. The poor little "exotics" had been fried in their beds. The hot manure was the cause of my trouble, even though the company of origin was correlated with the trouble.

There are some theorists who believe very firmly that early childhood sexual molesting has serious consequences to adult behavior and well-being. They would say there is a strong causation between the two events. Other theorists would say this implies correlation without necessarily implying causation.

Marty Seligman, the pioneer researcher in learned helplessness and learned optimism (see page 91), has surveyed the psychological literature on which issues we can control and change and which ones we can't. In his book, *What You Can Change and What You Can't*, he presents the results of his survey, showing that a predictable connection between early childhood experience and adult behaviors has not been established. There are numerous anecdotal accounts and even bodies of theoretical literature that draw the connection, but no scientific evidence. In fact, as we will see, his work on learned optimism grew out of his own findings that about one-third of the "victims" of horrific, abusive, and difficult experiences did not learn to be helpless, but rose above their circumstances and maintained an optimistic perspective on their lives.

Again, what does this have to do with child molesters?

Using early childhood trauma as an excuse for current adult behavior constitutes the "I'm a victim too" defense. Whether a victim of spouse abuse, child sexual abuse, or some other psychological trauma, the adult perpetrator excuses his or her behavior by blaming early childhood trauma. Yet, there are few people who have not suffered some type of trauma. Does that mean no one can be held accountable for his or her own actions?

While it is true that many molesters have been abused as children, most people who were abused never abuse children. Just because someone was abused as a child does not excuse or explain his becoming an abuser. We must still hold the person responsible and accountable for his behavior. We must also not be swayed by his victimization to treat him leniently, to decline to prosecute, to substitute treatment for incarceration, or to let him off because he holds a position of respect in the community.

Child molesters, especially preferential molesters, are dangerous, cunning criminals who prey on children. While we may not be able to stop them, we should take the responsibility for putting them away so they cannot continue to hurt more victims.

EXPLANATORY THEORIES OF MOLESTING BEHAVIOR

There are biological, psychological, and sociological theories of child molesting. Biological theories include addictions; psychological theories point to psychopathology; sociological theories include seeing molesters as ignorant or incompetent. An overarching, or inclusive, theory sees molesters as evil rather than physically or mentally ill.

The theory a person holds is closely tied to the treatment modality that is used. Twelve-step programs address molesting as a type of addiction. Psychologists and psychiatrists look to psychopathology, or mental or emotional illness, as the causative factor in molesting. Family therapists and sociologists look to social learning theory. And a disparate group is starting to look at child molesting as a manifestation of evil.

Let me reassure you that each of these theories has proponents and critics. These models are offered as a way for you to think through what you believe, what fits with your value structure, and, more importantly, how you view your own molesting spouse and the impact of his actions on your life. You probably already are using one of these models, and may not realize it. Be aware that the model you use shapes how you see him, yourself, and the options you think you have. When you finally embrace a model, you'll have a tendency to interpret your world, and that of everyone else, from this framework, whether it fits or not. Sometimes the consequences may be funny, other times they are very painful. So, be thoughtful about what theory you use and how you use it. Theories are powerful.

Sexual Addiction

With the increasing popularity of twelve-step/recovery programs, it has become common to label sexual acting out and sexual molesting of children as an addiction. The addiction model presents sexual acting out as a disease much like alcoholism or drug abuse. The disease model of addiction includes several commonly held beliefs, regardless of the type of addition that is being referred to:

- The disease is inbred and/or biological. Addiction is bred into you from birth or early childhood. Your current behavior, values, and beliefs have little if anything to do with whether or not you will lose yourself to the addiction.

- Addictions are forever. You may be in recovery but you will never be *recovered*. Addictions stay with you as long as you live. Once an addict, always an addict.

- The addiction is "progressive." If you continue to abuse the substance or person you are addicted to, your disease will inevitably get worse and worse, expanding until it takes over and destroys your whole life.

- Addictions require medical and/or spiritual treatment. You can't heal yourself. Willpower, personal growth, psychotherapy, relocating, or making changes in your life circumstances won't take care of the addiction.

Only medical treatment, with in-patient treatment in alcoholism or drug addiction units, or a twelve-step program such as Alcoholics Anonymous or special twelve-step programs for drug addiction, sex addiction, love addiction, or eating addiction, can provide the spiritual support and treatment necessary to stay in recovery from the disease on an ongoing basis.

Several twelve-step programs (such as Sex and Love Addicts Anonymous [SLAA] and Sex-Aholics Anonymous) have been formed to address the issues and the phenomenon that is becoming known as sexual addiction. These groups see sexual activity as compulsive, much like drinking is for the alcoholic, or drugs are for the drug addict. It is seen as a behavior over which the person has no control, an illness that can be controlled, but from which recovery is impossible.

Sex and Love Addicts Anonymous defines sexual addiction as:

*the use of a substance or activity for the purpose of lessening
pain or augmenting pleasure by a person who has lost control
over the rate, frequency, or duration of its use and whose life
has become progressively unmanageable as a result.*

It as an addiction not just because of the need to use sex and romance more than other people but because of the motives behind the use of sex and romance. The sexually addicted person, they say, uses sex to lessen the pain that comes from the problems in other areas of his or her life.

Author Patrick Carnes, a proponent of the addiction model of sexual acting out, talks about three stages of sexual addiction, each one more extreme in behavior and consequences in *Out of the Shadows.* The first level of sexual addiction he describes includes behaviors that are regarded as normal, acceptable, or tolerable, but used excessively. He includes masturbation, homosexuality, and prostitution in this category. Level two behaviors include behaviors that he sees as clearly victimizing, and for which legal sanctions are enforced. He classifies these as "nuisance" offenses such as exhibitionism or voyeurism. The level three behaviors are those that have grave consequences for the victims and potential legal consequences for the addicts, such as incest, child molestation, or rape. Carnes considers twelve-step programs the best treatment to recovery.

One of the most outspoken critics of the disease theory of addiction is psychologist Stanton Peele. In his book, *Truth About Addiction and Recovery,* Peele flatly states that not only is addiction *not* a disease, but both medical and twelve-step treatment programs are not effective in providing a cure. Instead, he sees an addiction as an ingrained habit that undermines the health, work, and relationships of an individual. He believes that many people who would have been classified with a substance abuse addiction have, in fact, grown out of that addiction as they matured and found other behavior patterns more effective or more rewarding. He also refers to the treatment outcome research that has shown that twelve-step programs are no more effective than having no treatment at all.

Peele also comments on how stigmatizing it is to label someone for life as "once an addict, always an addict." There is no opportunity to develop a concept of your life as someone other than an addict or an alcoholic or a codependent.

As a therapist, I find it distressing not only to label someone with a disease or by a term which by its nature is stigmatizing, but also to frame the treatment as recovery rather than healing. From a disease/addiction perspective, a person will always have the disease. It is with the person for the rest of his or her life. There is no sense of "getting over it." One can never not need ongoing support. What this implies is that people are unable to change and will always be dependent upon a twelve-step program or a therapist to live their lives. It keeps people dependent. It prevents people from accepting responsibility and accountability for their lives.

For spouses and family members, the impact of having a loved one "in recovery" can be dramatic. Many programs encourage daily meetings. Participants often spend considerable time with each other outside of meetings. The focus of a family's life can easily be characterized by meetings and long sessions with other participants, with a turning away from previous relationships and activities. Recovery programs can fill up the former addict's life.

> *Suzanne's husband had been fired from three hospital jobs for sexually molesting comatose patients he was supposed to be treating. He decided to go to SLAA to address his sexual addiction. Suzanne reported that not only did he constantly go to meetings where they talked of their sexual acting out, but he also spent hours on the phone with group members, talking about what they had done and what they wanted to do. Then, he starting inviting his new friends to their home.*
>
> *Suzanne threw him out when she came home one night to find a group of child molesters, rapists, and habitual masturbators sitting at her kitchen table. She was no longer willing to tolerate what she saw as his indulging himself in sexual fantasies and foibles.*

Framing sexual behavior as an addiction places the responsibility for sexual behavior outside of the person. He can blame his acting out on his "disease" rather than being challenged to accept the responsibility for his own sexual behavior. There is a tendency for people who are "addicted to sex" to deny there is anything they can do about it, or that they are responsible for their behaviors or the consequences of those behaviors. The addiction theory supports the molester's view of himself. It allows him to stay irresponsible and not change what he does. Sex controls him, he cannot control his sexual behavior.

Mental Illness

Many people are confused by mental illness. There are many different types of mental illness and many disagreements among mental health professionals about what causes mental illness, and what is the best treatment modality. In order to understand how mental illness could be the reason a person is a child molester it is necessary to discuss the varieties of conditions and behaviors that are classified as mental illness.

PSYCHOSIS: Psychosis is the most severe and least common form of mental illness. Psychotic people have lost touch with reality to the extent they can no longer live effectively in the world. They may report delusions, or beliefs that are not logical or rational, complain of hallucinations, or seeing or hearing things other people don't, and be self-destructive or try to hurt others. The current theory explaining psychosis is biological: there is a chemical imbalance or short circuit in the neurological mental functioning of the individual.

Marty was only six when she was molested by a man who lived in her neighborhood. Although her parents had forbidden her to play there, she was playing with a friend in a house under construction. The man, whom all the kids called Crazy Eddie, came into the house and scared the two little girls. Marty's friend ran screaming out into the yard. Marty tried to hide in the house, but Crazy Eddie found her, pulled down her panties, and fondled her. Marty never told

*her parents because she was afraid of being punished for not
obeying her parents' request to not go into the house.*

*As an adult, Marty was able to see that Crazy Eddie
was really psychotic. He lived in the garage of his family
home and was allowed to roam the neighborhood. She
reported he was finally institutionalized when she was in
junior high school. She doesn't know how many other kids
he had hurt by that time.*

NEUROSIS: Neurotics are painfully aware of reality. Whether experiencing symptoms of depression or anxiety, they typically hold themselves responsible for their own pain. Whatever other symptoms they report, shame and guilt are usually part of the package. They see themselves as the source of their own problems. Neurotics, with their overdeveloped consciences, don't make effective child molesters. Even if they are pedophiles, sexually attracted to children, they are too guilty to act out their attractions. They may watch children in public places, or look at pictures of children while they masturbate, but they don't usually act out directly with children.

*John lived in fear that he would be caught. He knew he
shouldn't be watching his campers shower after their swim,
especially since he got an erection every time he did. He was
sure he would never actually do anything, just watch. It was
both frightening and exciting, but he was most frightened of
being caught.*

Neurotic behavior is typically attributed to early family dysfunction, early relationship trauma, or inadequate parenting.

CHARACTER DISORDER: Character disordered individuals don't experience shame, guilt, or responsibility. They hold the rest of the world responsible for their pain. They see themselves as victims, regardless of what pain they cause others. Characteristics of character disordered individuals include being self-centered and insensitive to others, often lashing out in anger at others whom they blame. The situational molesting patterns of morally or sexually indiscriminate people are often described as character disordered. They don't seem to have the normal brakes and boundaries on their behaviors that others do. They act on their feelings, and then blame others for their actions.

Paul was furious when his stepdaughter complained to her mother about his attentions. Who did she think she was? She ran around the house in her skimpy nightie. It was an invitation and he took her up on it. It was her fault, not his. He ought to belt them both—the kid and her mother.

Character disorder is also usually attributed to early family dysfunction or relationship trauma. However, instead of developing too much conscience, character disordered individuals don't develop enough conscience. They feel entitled to get angry or to lash out at those whose behavior has inconvenienced them.

Mental Retardation
Mental retardation is not a mental illness. Most often caused by biological, or physical, factors, mental retardation is a lowered mental ability. Sometimes, but not always, a retarded individual will also experience emotional difficulties.

If this person molests a child, it would fit the inadequate pattern of situational molesting. While mentally retarded people may hang out around children in order to be sexual with them, they do not have the cognitive ability to develop the structure and predation necessary for a preferential molesting pattern.

Mack and Murphy thought it was great fun to sneak into the girl's bathroom when their care center group went to a museum. They wanted to see the girls with their pants down.

It is essential that retarded children and adults receive sex education information and training to insure that their curiosity and/or ignorance does not put them at risk.

Psychological Diagnosis and Therapy

In addition to understanding the types of psychological disorder a person may be experiencing, it is also important to understand the role of psychodiagnosis when it comes to treating people for psychological disorders.

To be treated, and to have that treatment paid for by insurance, a therapy patient must have a psychiatric diagnosis. According to the *Diagnostic and Statistical Manual of Mental Disorders* (DSM-III R), child molestation is usually diagnosed as one of two disorders: obsessive-compulsive disorder and/or pedophilia.

OBSESSIVE-COMPULSIVE DISORDER: Obsessive-compulsive disorder is described as repetitive, purposeful and intentional behaviors that are performed in response to an obsession, following certain rules, or stereotypical patterns. The obsession may be with delusions, illogical or unreal interpretations of the world around the person affected, or auditory hallucinations, hearing voices, or may fulfill some type of cultural, spiritual, sexual, or social needs of the patient.

Obsessions are thought patterns the individual struggles with. It is similar to hearing a song on the radio and then continuing to have it go through your head, over and over again. The difference is in intensity and duration. With an obsession, the thoughts aren't distracted by going to work, having the phone ring, or feeling hungry and needing to fix dinner. The obsession is strong and unrelenting.

Compulsions are actions. Some compulsive behaviors are trivial and may be the result of habit, superstition, or even safety considerations: feeling the button on the doorknob as you leave in the morning to make sure it is locked; not washing your lucky undershirt and wearing it to every game of the season; touching your hat, glove, knee, and elbow before pitching the ball.

Other compulsive behaviors are more serious and problematic: reciting elaborate word patterns before entering or leaving a room; washing your hands dozens of times in an evening; reciting a prayer or group of prayers nonstop during times of stress and discomfort. While there may not be anything "wrong" with any of these behaviors in and of themselves, it is the pattern of repetition and seeming lack of control over doing them, or the fear and foreboding of not doing them, that takes them over the line into compulsive behaviors. While most obsessions and compulsions are not sexual, obsessive-compulsive disorder is often used as a diagnosis for child molesters. This diagnosis is used because child molesters, especially preferential molesters, have strong, recurring thoughts and fantasies about sexual activities with children (obsessions) and act on those feelings (compulsions). The inference is that the child molester has no control over either his thoughts or feelings. He molests children because of his obsessive-compulsive disorder.

PEDOPHILIA: The other diagnostic category is pedophilia. Pedophilia occurs when there are recurrent, intense, sexual urges and sexually arousing fantasies of at least six months' duration, involving sexual activity with prepubescent children. The person has either acted on the urges or is markedly disturbed by them. "Children" is defined as generally thirteen years old or less; the age of the person is arbitrarily set at sixteen, or older, or at least five years older than the child.

A diagnosis of pedophilia only considers an individual's sexual preference, fantasies, and urges. It does not require that the person act on these urges, only that he is bothered by them. It also does not consider anything else about the person's life—how intelligent, educated, sensitive, hardworking, or nice he is. And he may be all of these and still be a pedophile.

As a psychological disorder, or mental illness, pedophilia is determined by fantasies, feelings, or behaviors. A person does not need to act on his feelings to be diagnosed as a pedophile. And, in fact, many people seek treatment so they won't act on these feelings and fantasies.

> *John entered into therapy because he was afraid he would act*
> *out his feelings more overtly. He was frightened he would*
> *progress from watching to trying to touch the boys. Being*
> *bothered by his feelings was enough to convince him he was*
> *on his way to being a pedophile.*

Most preferential molesters are not bothered by their feelings and fantasies of sexual activity with children. They seldom see the need to seek treatment. They don't think they are doing anything wrong. Even when professionals diagnose them as pedophiles, they reject the diagnosis.

If preferential molesters do enter into a treatment program it is usually because they have been arrested or imprisoned, and at that point they usually appear to cooperate with the treatment in an attempt to get a lighter sentence or to increase their opportunity for parole.

The Association for the Treatment of Sexual Abuse has been founded by a group of researchers and clinicians to both treat and do research on sexual offenders. Their goal is to change society's perception of sexual offenders as evil, untreatable, and hopelessly degenerate to one of people with a treatable disorder. They avoid the use of "shame-based" labels such as "pedophile" or "sexual deviant," helping their patients "realize they are simply misusing their sexuality or suffering from a sexual behavior problem."

Incompetent Parenting

It is hard to imagine parents who are so incompetent or unknowing that they hurt their children with sexual abuse, but there are certainly parents who fall into this category. These are the people who still don't realize that children might be harmed by having sexual relations with adults. Or, they have no sense that sex is an adult behavior rather than a behavior in which adults participate with children.

If incest and/or sexual child abuse has not been part of your personal experience, your reaction to the previous paragraph may well be one of shock and disbelief. Surely, you'll say, there could be no parents who are so unknowing or abusive. I can remember when I would have agreed with you, and when I was disabused of this notion. I was a student in a class on the psychology of women, many years before I found out about my husband. We were discussing incest. I had little to say. Not only had I never thought about it, I was sure no one I knew had ever experienced it. Then one of the women in the group commented in an offhand manner how common incest is, saying, "If she wasn't good enough for pa, what good was she?" And the woman next to me, with tears in her eyes, angrily muttered "none." And I knew I knew someone who was a victim of incest.

In some families sexual abuse is just one more way that parents or stepparents hurt their children. These situational abusers may combine sexual abuse with other physical and/or emotional abuse. Parents may drink or do drugs first, and be "so high" they "didn't know" what they were doing, or feel entitled to take a "power" position in the family, taking what they want from those less able to stand up for themselves.

Sometimes sexual abuse can rise out of the parents' lack of appropriate adult relationships, and they turn to their children as lovers.

After years of bitter quarreling, Walter's parents were divorced when he was eleven. Because his father worked the swing shift, he spent most of his time with his mom. She worked as a receptionist, barely making minimum wage. She lived in a very small apartment, with one bedroom and one bed. Walter's mother slept in the same bed with her son and fondled him until he was in his third year of high school. He never told anyone, especially his father. Then one day his dad came by to return some forgotten school books and found out about the sleeping arrangements. He demanded Walter come live at his house.

Now, as an adult, Walter has a hard time talking about what happened with his mother. He has never dated much, has not married, and still gets caught up in his mother's seductive behavior. She continues to see him as "her man" rather than her son. And he finds it very difficult to resist her requests for favors and to spend time with her rather than friends his own age.

This category of abusers corresponds to the FBI category of situational abusers. These are people who are not pedophiles, are not primarily sexually attracted to children, but molest them nonetheless.

Evil

I started to consider the concept of evil as I struggled to deal with my own situation. From the evidence I saw, it was clear that my husband had been molesting young boys for a number of years. Yet, when I confronted him, when the police arrested him, and when he was confronted by his victims and their legal representatives, he claimed to be innocent. He insisted that everyone was picking on him, and was very persistent and persuasive in trying to convince us all we were wrong and he was right. I started questioning my own perceptions, reactions, and beliefs.

The breakthrough for me came when I read Scott Peck's *The People of the Lie*. Best known for his best-seller, *The Road Less Traveled*, Peck turned to examining human evil in *The People of the Lie*. Drawn to the topic by witnessing the impact evil people have on their victims and how difficult it is to confront human evil, Peck looks at evil as it exists in everyday actions and activities.

I resisted the idea of human evil. The very idea that people might be evil was hard for me to deal with. Couple the notion of evil with molestation and the issue becomes even more problematical. It is difficult to speak of evil without conjuring up images of the devil, satanic cults, and ritualistic witchcraft and black magic. That is not what I am talking about here. Rather the evil molesters do is more individual and more subtle, if anything, more pervasive.

There has never not been evil. It exists in every religion, every mythology, every culture. Evil has been attributed to acts of God or Satan, random acts of nature, and/or acts that people purposefully commit and must answer for. From a religious perspective, theologians, pastors, and the faithful have struggled with resolving the paradox of evil with the concept of an all-powerful, benevolent God. The faithful and the profane have struggled to understand seemingly random destructive events: volcanic eruptions, earthquakes, storms, viruses, and accidents.

On a more human level, philosophers and village sages have described the potential for evil that exists in each of us. We all have the ability to choose evil: to dehumanize others and rationalize our actions toward them as we move forward in national conflicts or more privately as we manipulate and control others for our own needs. The issue is not "Is there evil?" but "How do I deal with the evil within me?" Child molesters don't deal with this issue. They deny their evil, and this makes them even more dangerous.

Evil is one of the most difficult things for victims to cope with because evil behavior is very subtle, covert, and persistent. The evil person does not acknowledge or admit to what he is doing, and does not recognize that what he is doing is harmful. He presents himself as faultless, and does not own his behavior. He may scapegoat, or blame others, for what he did. Molester Ross Nelson blames both the boys he molested and their parents. If the parents had been more available or had done a better job teaching their sons good moral values, the boys would not have succumbed to his advances. It wasn't his fault.

Some molesters use projection, or see in others what they are unwilling to see in themselves. They try to maintain an appearance of moral purity and perfection, while easily seeing their same faults in others. Ironically, they are not motivated to be good, but to appear to be good. They live a life of pretense, a life of lies.

> *Elmo was a self-proclaimed children's champion. Whenever there was an incident of child molesting, a conference on sexual abuse, or pending legislation, Elmo was there with an angry, verbose contribution on the evils of others. A self-styled "counselor," he was typically accompanied by a young boy whom he had rescued from a life of depravity. The boy would live with Elmo while Elmo "treated" him. There was no one more committed to helping kids than he was, Elmo would say.*
>
> *After watching him deliver a paper at a conference one day, I casually mentioned to the police officer sitting next to me how tireless Elmo seemed to be for the cause. The police officer laughed out loud and then told me of the extensive kiddy porn collection Elmo had, "for research" Elmo claimed, and the officer drew my attention to how familiar Elmo was in touching the boy he was currently helping. With a sinking heart, I realized what all of his righteous indignation and judgments of others were covering in himself.*

Molesters go to great lengths to maintain their appearance of purity, hiding from even those closest to them their evil acts. This secrecy makes it less likely they will be caught and easier to deny what they have been doing when they do get caught. The evil person, not acknowledging the nature of his behavior, projecting his problem onto others, also sees no need to change or to seek treatment. Since there is no problem, why get treatment? These molesters won't take steps to change or verbalize a willingness to change unless there is a secondary gain, such as getting or staying out of jail. Then they "go through the motions" until the pressure is off and they can return to their previous way of being. When they are remanded to treatment as a condition of their sentencing, the dropout rate is high, and even if they do finish the treatment program, the recidivism rate is high. They re-offend as soon as they have the chance.

At the same time the evil person is denying what he does, scapegoating or projecting onto others, he is purposefully gathering new victims and their families and unsuspecting acquaintances under his control. One spouse of a child molester described how charismatic her husband was. He could quickly gather a group of children with him no matter where he went. The children became enthralled with him, preferring to be with him rather than other children or their own families.

Thrall is a very powerful concept and experience. Child molesters count on it not only to control their child victims but to deceive their spouses, friends, and family and to dislodge their critics. Child molesters, especially preferential molesters, are sly and cunning. They are seductive toward others, not only in a sexual sense but in winning commitment from and connection with others. Using all their skills at assessing what others need, the seducers present themselves as the answer to those needs. Like chameleons who change color to match their environment, molesters match the needs and expectations of their targeted victims. Waging a subtle, persistent campaign, they draw others to them, holding the others in thrall. Even when later evidence of wrongdoing or deception is present, the connections between the abusers and their victims are so strong, it is difficult to break through. They are like wicked witches who put their targets under a magic spell. And mere mortals cannot break that spell.

Child molesters foster the dependency of the children, seeking to control them and use them for their own needs. They have little feelings for what is best or even good for the children. They only see their own purposes. It is as if the world and, more specifically, other people exist only for their use. They dehumanize their victims, family, friends, and colleagues. It is a form of noxious narcissism.

We all have some form of narcissism, seeming to care so much for ourselves that we cut out or shut out others. Being so self-absorbed makes relationships difficult and transitory. We use others to get what we want. The evil person pushes that narcissism to the extreme, not only disregarding others, but treating them as if they were unworthy of notice, as if they were things, objects, not people. By objectifying others he denies even their basic humanity.

The question remains, what do we gain by characterizing child molesters as evil? It is necessary to consider both the molester and his victims when addressing this question.

From a molester's perspective, considering him as evil cuts off the opportunity of treatment. If a person is characterized as evil, there is little hope treatment will be effective. The Association for Treatment of Sexual Abusers holds the view that sexual deviance is a disorder, not an evil. They see themselves as professional healers, able to work with sexual deviants, not judge them or respond in a punitive way. Because they see deviance as a disorder, they believe treatment is not only appropriate but has some likelihood of success. However, they also admit the treatment is long, the road is arduous for both the therapist and patient, and the dropout rate and instances of reoffending high.

But, the effectiveness of treatment is not the issue. Few molesters voluntarily come for treatment. Treatment can only be mandated if the molester enters the judicial system, either through a child protective services complaint or a criminal complaint. Most molesters never get into the system, and don't go for treatment on their own.

The evil person molests or hurts the child out of a sense of entitlement and feelings of bringing pleasure to himself from the child's pain. A major characteristic of these people is to absolutely deny or discount the evilness of their motivations or behavior. Nonetheless, their behavior is destructive toward their intended victims.

Although there may be a few cases in which child molesting is the consequence of an incompetent or uneducated adult, or a form of mental illness of psychosexual immaturity, more commonly professionals view child molesters as character disordered or evil.

Mark excused his attraction to and involvement with young boys by saying he was just doing what men have been doing since the time of the Greeks. The most noble form of love he said was that between a man and a boy. He was a proud member of the Man Boy Love Association, and took particular pride and delight in inducting new, young members.

Sam had different reasons. He blamed his involvement with young girls on the media first, and his wife second. What was a man to do? he would ask. All these ads that showed children in sexually provocative poses. He couldn't help it. They enticed me, he would say. Besides, his wife was busy with the new baby, and not as available as he would have liked.

For the victims—the children, the spouses, and other family and friends—characterizing child molesters as evil has great significance and impact.

First, seeing child molestation as evil puts the responsibility for the molester's actions back on the molester. We can see child molestation as a choice some people make: a choice to act on their feelings. By acknowledging that every one of us is capable of evil, but only some of us act on those feelings, we hold accountable those who act on their destructive urges.

Putting the responsibility on the molester debunks the myth that women marry molesters because of their own co-dependency, that a woman chooses to marry a molester, or that a child chooses to be molested. The evil is his, not theirs. They were in the wrong place at the wrong time. The distress and anguish the victims experience are predictable consequences of extreme, continuous, noxious stress, not mental disorders of their own making.

Second, seeing molestation as an evil that has insinuated into the molester's life, for which there is little hope of change and for which even the most skilled therapists have poor outcome results, reinforces for the spouse that there is little if anything she can do to make a difference—either in her marriage or in her mate. Not only won't he change, but he will continually lie to her about what he is doing and who he is.

Third, seeing a child molester as evil allows the victim to deal with the abuse and the abuser as discrete experiences that were caused by one bad man, and not generalize the abuse as something all youth group leaders, parents, fathers, uncles, or coaches do. What this means for the victim is that she has the potential for having relationships with other men in these roles and does not have to fear there will always be an ogre hiding in the attic.

Chapter 3

Don't Blame Me

Why does man, in contrast to the animal world, have problems?

— C. G. JUNG, *Modern Man in Search of a Soul*

Being married to a child molester is no one's plan A for her life. For most women, the news of their mates' behavior comes as a surprise. Yet they quickly start to question themselves.

> Anne was not all that surprised when her husband was arrested for child molesting. She knew something was going on, and was pretty sure he was being "crazy" with the kids. An angry and violent man, he had often beaten her when she tried to talk to him about his behavior. She had learned long ago to look away and protect herself and her kids as best she could. She knew it was only a matter of time before something really serious would get him in trouble with the law.
>
> For Tanisha, the issue was not just what he did—but how he could have done it to her. Seeing herself as educated and sophisticated, she knew no one in her family had ever

done anything like this. How could he be so stupid? But then,
she asked, wasn't it just like a man, thinking he could do
whatever he wanted to do, with anyone he wanted to do it to?

Women like Anne and Tanisha need and want to know how they ever got into this position in the first place. *How could my life turn out this way?* is a common question. So many women look to self-help literature, self-help groups, or therapy to help them find an understanding of how this awful thing happened to them.

THE ROLE OF THEORY

Sociological and psychological research has had much to say about women, about victims, and about abusers. Not all of it is consistent; some studies and theories are directly in opposition to others. In these cases, it is difficult to know what is "true." Sometimes, multiple explanations for the same situation can all have a kernel of truth in them. People react differently to situations. What might be true for one person is not true at all for another. The challenge is to review what others have said, and then determine what is true for you.

A word of warning though. If an issue, theory, or model is making you very confused, or very angry, do not just dismiss it. Come back to it at a later time. Talk it through with a friend or member of your support team, reread the passage you found troublesome, have a dialogue with yourself about what this means for you. Consider the part that might be true, or the part that might fit your situation. When an idea triggers such strong feelings, it can be a signal that it fits, even though we don't want it to, or even if it is unattractive.

For example, at one point in my own journey I was participating in a support group that consisted primarily of women who had been sexually abused as children. Several of the members were adamant that I had to have been abused myself, or I would not have chosen a husband who seventeen years later turned out to be a molester. I dismissed their charges. "Don't be ridiculous," I said, "my father would have never done something like that." My denials made them all crazy. They were sure I was blocking the experience. I had to have been abused. They were more sure of my early childhood experience than I was.

So I thought more carefully about it. I reviewed my childhood memories. I reviewed some of the painful memories and experiences I had. I talked to my sisters about their early memories. I heard about an uncle and a cousin who had fondled both of them. I had never spent much time with those relatives, so I escaped the groping fingers. After thinking it through, I am sure I was never molested as a child. The women in my support group still believe I am blocking the memories of certain childhood sexual abuse.

This experience mirrors the experiences of several other spouses of child molesters, and, in fact, other therapy clients I have worked with. When a situation fills your life, it colors how you interpret your world. It is hard to imagine that other people don't see the world the way you do. It's easy to believe that what is true for you must be true for others.

WIFE BLAMING

The most common reaction people have when they hear of a case of child molesting, especially by a spouse or other family member, is to blame the wife of the molester. Just as mothers are held accountable for behavioral problems of their children, wives are held accountable for the sexual behavior of their husbands.

The "conventional wisdom" is that the wife knows about the sexual abuse and either encourages her spouse or doesn't protect her children from the abuser. Some theorists and therapists even talk about the wife and mother as the "silent partner" in the abuse, insisting that she is a participant whether she knows about the abuse or not.

All too often therapists and recovery groups encourage victims of child sexual abuse to hold their mothers accountable for their father's abuse. At a large conference on organized religion and child sexual abuse, much attention was given to protecting the feelings and issues of the victims of child sexual abuse. I sat in a darkened auditorium listening to speaker after speaker recount stories of their abuse. Both men and women bravely told of the terrible things that had been done to them. And then, they railed against their mothers for knowing and not doing anything about it.

I was astounded. Virtually every woman I had treated did not know of her spouse's abuse. Yet these victims were certain their mothers not only knew of, but went along with, the abuse. They were so careful to protect each victim's own feelings, but were not aware of how abusive they were being toward their mothers. They could only think of their own pain, and they had little if any awareness of the pain and the betrayal their mothers had experienced.

I wish I could say I stood up and shouted they were wrong. That we were victims too. But I didn't. I couldn't face their rage. I didn't want them all to direct it toward me.

So, I went home and cried.

This pattern repeated itself numerous times. During each conference I attended, the rage and abuse heaped on the spouse of the child molester was as great, if not greater, than the rage directed at the abuser himself. Participants would relate stories of incest, instances of being molested by family friends or relatives, and then rage at their mothers for not preventing the attack, for not believing them when they told of an incident, or for discounting the severity or consequences of the attack. Seldom if ever did an adult who had been victimized as a child tell of a mother who was supportive, took action to remedy a situation, or accept the accusation of abuse as true.

One conference participant reported that his mother was to blame for the breakup of his family. When she found out his father was sodomizing him and his brother, she reported the father to protective services, filed for divorce, and took the children and moved back to her hometown in a distant state. He didn't blame his abusing father, but his mother who was acting to protect her children. It was as if it were safer somehow to blame his mother for standing by, rather than his father for being so evil and hurtful.

The concept of not protecting the child from sexual abuse assumes that the wife knows about the abuse and that she is in a position to take action against her abusing spouse. Yet, many of the wives themselves have been victims of early abuse, continue to be abused by their husbands, and are struggling to maintain their own sanity and well-being. It is unconscionable that we should hold these women responsible for not only taking care of their children, for not functioning at a high enough level to be effective managers of their families, often while holding an outside job, for being subjected to their husbands' abuse, and for not being able to prevent them from continuing to abuse their children and themselves. We expect the wives to know what is purposely being kept secret, to protect the children from an unknown evil act, and to continue to carry out her everyday responsibilities as if nothing was happening. Few women can be that omniscient, strong, and competent in the face of unrelenting abuse. What is worse, the incesting fathers are then treated sympathetically by their child victims, as well as by the community, because the mothers pushed their children on them, or were unavailable for their husbands' needs. It is time we started making the offenders responsible for their own behavior and stopped blaming the wives and mothers.

Unconscious Involvement

In *Betrayal of Innocence*, psychologist Susan Forward says she believes not all wives are aware of the incest or involved in it. But of the majority of wives who are involved, she says only a few are consciously involved. Most of them are unconsciously involved. In other words, a wife may not know anything about the abuse, and yet she is responsible and has played a role in allowing it to happen. She is held responsible not because she actively did anything, but because she unconsciously supported and allowed her husband to hurt their children. He actively abuses the children but is not held responsible. She doesn't know about the abuse but is held responsible. Forward falls into the same pattern, blaming one of the victims, not the perpetrator. She holds a wife responsible for her husband's sexual behavior.

The most common reason offered for wives encouraging their husbands' abuse is to avoid being sexual themselves. They offer their daughters so they won't have to have sexual relations with their spouses. This perspective perpetuates the view that the wives of child molesters are sexually repressed or want to avoid sex relations. Yet spouses of child molesters commonly report it is their husbands, not they, who avoid marital relations.

Choosing to Marry a Molester

Physician Jennifer Schneider, in *Back from Betrayal*, a book about women who marry men who are sexually addicted, speaks to this point. The cover of the book proclaims that you are "not alone and not to be shamed or blamed" if you have married a man who is sexually addicted. Then she goes on to say of such women:

> We also need to recognize that we have not been entirely innocent victims . . . . A woman rarely marries a sex addict by accident. She usually has clues before marriage of the problems to come but does not dwell on them. She expects him to make her happy and then becomes resentful when he fails to live up to her expectations. Accepting our share of the responsibility for our hurt will help us to forgive our partner.

Schneider suggests several risk factors that account for women choosing to marry sex addicts, including a heightened awareness of sexuality in the family of origin, early sexual experience with peers or other abuse, and a belief that sex is the most important sign of love. She describes women who marry child molesters as sick, addicted, and out of control. They chose to be married to sex addicts.

As I was writing this book, an acquaintance from where I used to live came to town. She called and we met for dinner. She knew little of my personal history. Over dinner conversation she asked me what I was doing. When I told her about the book, and my husband being a child molester, her reaction was to say with disbelief, "You chose to marry a child molester?"

When I replied that I didn't know he was a molester when I married him, she kept insisting I did know and I purposely chose to marry him because I somehow needed to go through this experience.

No matter what I said, she kept saying there is no such thing as coincidence, I knew what I was getting into, and I had to stop seeing him as bad or evil. The problems I had had nothing to do with him or what he did. I alone was responsible, because I chose to marry a molester.

Finally, in frustration, I asked her if she believed that the children who were molested chose to be molested. Of course, she said. Then she went on to qualify that the desire or need to be molested may have been unconscious, but it was the children's need to be hurt that brought this event into their lives. Is this crazy or what? She did not hold the molester responsible for hurting people, but did hold his victims responsible for being hurt.

At one point during my recovery process I attended a popular self-help seminar. In a large hotel ballroom, the facilitator spoke about personal responsibility to the 250 people that were assembled. The catchphrase he used was, "What did you do to promote, enable, and allow this condition to occur in your life?" First an implication and then a direct statement from the facilitator declared that anything you were experiencing you brought on yourself. No one else was responsible for any of the pain you were having in your life. It was up to you to accept the responsibility for allowing or enabling the difficult experiences you had.

So, how did I, how did we, get here?

Lust and Insanity

I surely don't believe that we consciously or unconsciously chose to marry child molesters, anymore than I believe children choose to be molested. In *The Mirage of Marriage*, William Lederer and Don Jackson, two marriage theorists from Stanford University, characterize courtship as a time of lust and insanity. The insanity is characterized by trying to make yourself fit the ideal expectations of your potential mate so he will want to marry you. You try to be who he thinks you should be, and, most importantly, he tries to convince you he is who you want. Both partners, in their attempts to please and woo one another, present a false image of who they are, and discount any suggestion that the other isn't who he or she is pretending to be. When you're in love, you see your lover through rose-colored glasses.

Lust is the driving force of the chemistry between two lovers, convincing both of them that their hearts and hormones know the truth. Lust bypasses rational thought and decision-making. You choose to marry the one you love and lust after. To expect anyone to see all the faults of the other is unreasonable, especially if that person is as cunning and manipulative as a child molester.

I was more than ready to get married when I met my husband. Looking back on my decision I realize part of my motivation to attend graduate school was to meet a husband. We were introduced by a mutual friend at the beginning of my first year of graduate school. We dated steadily and exclusively for six or seven months, and then he invited me to come meet his parents over spring break. He proposed to me during that vacation and we set the date for the fall.

What attracted me to him? He was one of the smartest men I had ever met. We could talk for hours, we played word games, and we made each other laugh. He would leave a flower on my desk, he would call me the minute the football game was over on Sunday afternoon, and he told me he loved me—and wanted me to share his life. The flat sides? He was too serious. Sometimes, he would get into a rut and not want to get out of it, but he helped with my Sunday school class and worked with the teens at the church. We went camping, hiking, and canoeing, and talked for hours and hours and hours. I didn't marry a child molester. The person I married turned out to be a child molester.

I didn't make him a child molester. Neither are you responsible for turning your spouse into a child molester. This is not to say you were the perfect wife. No one is. We all make mistakes. To tell the truth, I am strong, loud-mouthed, and assertive—to the point of being aggressive sometimes. But, my behavior, character, or style was not the determining factor in my husband molesting young boys. Was he affected by who I am? Of course he was. Just as I have been affected by him. But I am no more responsible for his sexual acting out than he is for "ruining my life."

The difference is, he did molest children and my life isn't ruined. Certainly I didn't plan on marrying a child molester, I didn't want it to happen. I was angry when it did, but I also decided that I could go on and not let him, and what he did, decide if I was going to be happy or depressed, a success or a failure, a good mother or a bad one. Those were up to me—not him. And it took me a long time before I realized this and felt ready to take the steps necessary to work on my life.

Her Frigidity, His Excuse

When situations of child sexual abuse become known in the community, through newspaper or television stories, it is not uncommon to hear comments such as "If the wife had been available, the man wouldn't have needed to turn to children."

Max claimed he had molested his daughter when his wife was ill and sexually unavailable. He excused his behavior, saying he would have been committing adultery if he had sex with his neighbor, and his religion said that adultery was a sin. Since his daughter was part of his family, he wasn't really committing adultery.

What is remarkable about his perspective is that Max considered the women in his family as property—belonging to him, available for satisfying his sexual needs. His right was to have a sexual outlet, whether his wife was available or not.

Men who are sexually involved outside of their marriage often use the common rationale that the wife is frigid. If she seems unavailable or unwilling, the man has the right to extracurricular sexual activity. He is entitled, because she is not upholding her end of the contract. Or, in my case, an acquaintance said my husband was justified in acting out sexually because I was too strong and assertive. He told me, in all seriousness, if I was less outgoing, and more submissive, my husband would not have been forced to turn to young boys for his sexual partners.

Yet, when spouses of child molesters are asked about their sexual feelings and behaviors, they typically report no problem with marital sexual relations. In fact, they either report having sexual relations fairly regularly with their spouses, or if there is a low drive issue, it is his not theirs. This underscores the notion that a person's sexual behavior is his or her own responsibility, *not* the responsibility of his or her partner.

Therapists and social service workers, judges and divorce lawyers, subscribe to this same conventional wisdom. They often see the wives as encouraging and knowing about the sexual abuse, or making unfounded accusations to support their malicious desires to deny their soon-to-be former spouses custody of the children.

A pamphlet published by a professional nursing association flatly states that wives know about child sexual abuse, see it as a relief for themselves, organize time for their daughters to be alone with their fathers, and will not risk exposing the abuse.

It wasn't just my divorce lawyer who discounted my allegations of my husband's sexual abuse. Many lawyers believe women tend to cloud the issues of divorce with unfounded charges. It is then up to a woman to convince her lawyer that the charges she makes are true. The attorney's assumption is it couldn't possibly be true. So she has two tasks: getting a divorce and convincing her attorney she's telling the truth.

FAMILY SYSTEMS THEORY AND THERAPY

Family systems theory and therapy is an approach many marriage and family counselors use to treat people within the context of their families. From this perspective, the family operates as a unit with each person affecting and being affected by each other. When considering abuse or family violence, this theory suggests that both the abuser and the victim play a role in the behavior. Taken to extremes, this view reinforces these perceptions of the abuse, and mandates that the abuser alone is not at fault. The man can either share the blame with the victim, or his spouse. A typical response could be:

> *If she hadn't bounced on my lap, I wouldn't have been aroused. When she does that, what am I supposed to do? I couldn't help myself. It was her fault. She excited me. Besides, my wife won't have sex with me as often as I need to.*

Incest: Who Knows?

From a family systems perspective, there is no uninvolved person in any problematic family situation. The assumption is the wife/mother knows and condones incestuous relations. But this discounts the ability many people have for keeping secrets from their spouses. Many people have sexual affairs with consenting adults and keep them from their spouses for many years. The wives are often the last to know.

Child molesters are extremely manipulative, and are usually very successful at keeping their deviant behavior a secret from everyone other than their victims. To hold a wife responsible for behavior she did not know about and, in fact, was being intentionally kept from her, is outrageous at best.

Eleanor was astounded to learn of her adult daughter's claim of sexual abuse. All of her girls had seemed so close to their father. She had no idea that he had gotten up out of their bed in the middle of the night to slip into their daughter's beds. The few times she was aware of his being gone, his explanation of using the bathroom made enough sense for her to never suspect. After one daughter came forward, the other two admitted he had molested them as well. The girls had never even talked about it among themselves.

Janet's father threatened her not to tell her mother about how he "punished" her. When she only got A's instead of A+'s on her report card, he would take her into the bedroom, close the door, take her clothes off, and whip her. He pinched her breasts and put his fingers into her vagina. She tried to defy him, but he told her that her mother would find out and it would kill her mother to know what a nasty girl she was.

Now as an adult Janet realizes her father was the nasty one, and her mother was terrified of him and the whippings he gave her. Janet finally stopped blaming her mother for her father's evil ways.

Janet still will not tell her mother what her father did, and is concerned that her mother will find out. She is sure that her father's threats are accurate. It will kill her mother to know. Janet is just now starting to understand the maliciousness of his behavior. He coerced her into keeping his secret, and allowed Janet to blame her mother for failing to protect her from him. Without knowing what was going on, Janet's mother was at fault.

Responsive to/Responsible for

There is no question that family members are influenced by the feelings or behaviors of one other. It is impossible to live in close quarters with someone without having the feelings, the moods, the behaviors of the other person directly impact how you are thinking or feeling. However, when I work with couples or with families in therapy, I carefully point out that, while it is important to be responsive to the needs, behaviors, and feelings of the other persons, you can't be responsible for them.

Each adult is responsible for his or her own behavior, especially his or her sexual behavior, regardless of what is going on in the family or with other family members. So if the child snuggles on her father's lap and the father finds it arousing, the arousal is not the child's responsibility. The father is responsible for his feelings and it is up to him to define the boundaries and to make a decision about how to respond appropriately. When an adult puts the responsibility on the child for being seductive, the appropriate reaction is to tell the man to act like the adult he is. It is up to him to manage the situation no matter how the child acts.

Oftentimes people react to their perceptions of what their role should be, rather than to the particular individual who is fulfilling that role. What this means is that *anyone* a molester happened to marry would be seen as at fault, wrong, or the cause of his difficulties.

> *As Mark and Joanne's marriage started to experience some difficulties, Mark quickly ascribed the blame to Joanne's inability to relax. Mark claimed things would be just fine if she would just "loosen up a bit." He was particularly angry at her because she didn't like the social activities he did. Specifically, she didn't like to go to X-rated movies. This issue became a bone of contention between the two of them as they attempted to make plans for each weekend.*

After much soul-searching, Joanne finally went to her pastor, asking his advice on how to be both a good wife and uphold her moral standards. The pastor encouraged her to be a compliant wife and to respect her husband's wishes as the head of the household.

With some misgivings, she decided it wouldn't hurt to go to the movies her husband liked. She hoped if they went, maybe he would get it out of his system, and then they could go on to other social activities. As they started to plan for the next weekend, she told him she would be willing to do whatever he wanted. He could make their plans. He didn't believe her. When she tried to reassure him that she would go to any movie he wanted to go to, his reaction surprised her. He turned away from her for a moment and when he turned back, he was livid. He pointed his finger at her nose, and in a loud, angry voice claimed it was all her fault their marriage was failing. She had no integrity, she would not stand up for what she believed, but instead she was willing to acquiesce. That was why he didn't love her anymore.

Joanne was in a no-win situation. No matter what she did, she was to blame for his anger. Mark was hurting and angry for his own reasons, reasons that had virtually nothing to do with which movie they saw on Saturday night. Anything she did would be cause for him to be angry at her. He was angry and, no matter what she did, he would get more angry.

Mark's anger was there long before she made her decision about the movies she wanted to see. Did she have a *role* in his anger? Absolutely. Was she the *cause* of his anger? In no way.

In families, the need of one person for another to behave in a particular way may be invisible to both involved. Mark needed to be angry and needed to see Joanne as the cause of his anger. So he developed a whole image of what he thought she was and how she was responsible for his anger. His beliefs and image of her bore no relation to what she thought she was or what she thought she was trying to do.

The results of his fantasy allowed him to continue to be angry and not to acknowledge any responsibility for his anger.

In her research on over three hundred cases of sexual abuse, Kathleen Coulbourn Faller, Ph.D., from the University of Michigan School of Social Work, found wives typically do not know of the abuse, and, when they do know, they bring it out into the open and take steps to make it stop. The result is the destruction of the two-parent family. When a wife doesn't report the abuse, it is because she is being victimized herself or is too afraid of her husband to speak out. In either event the wife faces being blamed: if she leaves she is blamed for breaking up the family; if she stays she is labeled co-dependent and criticized for not protecting her children from her husband's abuse.

It is unrealistic to assume that even if the spouse did know about the behavior, she would be able to control the molester's behavior or stop him from doing it. In most marriages, it is impossible to change the behavior of a spouse with regard to trivial matters such as table manners and picking up dirty clothes, much less more substantive issues such as substance abuse and gambling. It is unreasonable to expect that a spouse could control her partner's sexual behavior, even if she did know about it.

Chapter 4

The Initial Reactions

I realized that if my agony was to be ameliorated, I had to face my fear and surrender to the hurting.
— SHELDON KUPP, M.D.
Raise Your Right Hand Against Fear

There is no one pattern of reaction or experience you go through when you are married to a child molester. So much of what happens is out of your hands. A lot depends on what he did, who knows about the abuse, what children are involved and how you view your marriage, your responsibilities, and your options.

Sometimes the knowledge of the molesting does not appear until many years later, even after the molester is dead. Other times, you will be the one who discovers what he is doing or find out from family or friends. There may have been a single incident, or multiple incidents with multiple victims. In hindsight you may be able to look back and see the signs of the abuse, but this clarity of vision is seldom visible at the time the abuse occurs or in foresight.

Although the patterns may vary, the shared experience is one of pain and grief. No matter what he did, or how you react, there will be pain and grief. At the same time their lives are being turned upside down because of their husbands' behavior, most spouses of child molesters report being held responsible for what they did, and as being the target of anger from his family, their own family and friends, and, most of all, from the children he hurt.

Feelings and Experiences

It is difficult to sort out your feelings when you learn your spouse is a child molester. A personal crisis like this will act like a web that insinuates itself into all the different parts of your life. Feeling ambivalent, feeling that you must be crazy, denying that it could ever possibly have happened, and then just dealing with the logistics of what is happening in your life right now can be extremely difficult no matter what your personal circumstances.

Denial

The most common initial reaction is denial. It couldn't be happening. It must be a bad dream. Things like this don't happen to me. I know I'm going to wake up and find out this is just a bad dream. This initial denial is a combination of "It can't be true" and "I don't want it to be true."

> Expecting her second child in two months, Lorraine went to stay with her parents and five-year-old sister while her husband was out of town on a temporary work assignment. After the little ones were in bed, her mother poured another cup of coffee and then spilled the news. Lorraine's husband had molested her little sister, Sally, numerous times.
>
> Sally had missed her big sister after she got married and, over the summer, had come to spend weekends with her. Sally would arrive Saturday mornings, spend the night, and Lorraine would take her to church on Sunday mornings.

Lorraine was horrified. But, as she listened to her mother, acknowledged the changes in her sister, and thought over the visits, she realized he had ample opportunity. He would offer to baby-sit Sally while Lorraine went shopping, offered to bathe Sally, was sure to check she was covered up before they went to sleep.

Looking further back, she remembered his unreasonable jealousy when she made an appointment with a male doctor, his verbal and physical abuse when he was drinking, his offering to change their daughter's diaper even though she wasn't wet. When Lorraine confronted him, her husband not only confessed to molesting her sister, but their own daughter as well.

Lorraine was completely paralyzed from the shock. She stumbled through the days in a fog, watching her sister's pain, giving birth to her son, and letting her mother care for them all. Meanwhile the state stepped in and prosecuted her husband, found him guilty, and sentenced him to up to fifteen years in prison.

Nothing broke through Lorraine's fog until her mother threatened to put her children in foster care. She started seeing a therapist, and dealing with her hurt and anger. Eventually Lorraine decided on divorce, even though her church only allowed divorce in the case of adultery. She considers what he did to her sister adultery. Even though she said she still loved him, she considered him mentally ill and a threat to both her and their children.

Like many other spouses of child molesters, Lorraine went through a period of feeling victimized by his behaviors. Friends and acquaintances told her it was against God's will to give up on him, that he was a nice guy who only did what he did because she wasn't "giving him any." And then a social worker told her 98 percent of sex offenders repeat their offenses and Lorraine knew she had made the right decision.

As the story unfolds, you will probably keep uncovering new information about what has been going on and the sense that it could be true becomes stronger and stronger, until finally it is undeniable. Or, like the woman in the next story, you might not recognize the abuse, or accept it in its entirety. However, most women say they move from their denial to a very clear sense of the reality of the situation.

> *Estelle is sure her husband is not guilty of the crimes he has been convicted of. She says her daughter, who accused her father of rape and sodomy, and who testified against her father, is sick and confused. She has called on God to exorcise the evil spirits from her daughter.*
>
> *Estelle does say that her husband fondled the girl. But she denies intercourse ever happened, even though medical evidence showed otherwise. He was convicted of eight of nine counts and was sentenced to life plus twenty years in prison. (He will be eligible for parole in seven years.)*
>
> *Estelle believes any judgment of her husband is for God, not the state, to make. Since he has repented, his slate is washed clean. She feels he has made his peace and been forgiven by God, so he should be forgiven by the state.*

Estelle no longer denies the incident, but she denies the severity of the abuse and continues to want to act as if it is all over. She is still denying his civil responsibility, acting as if his spiritual forgiveness should be enough of a "solution" to his abuse.

Anger

It is a fine line between anger and rage. Anger is the "I don't like this, I want it different and I want it different right now" feeling. Rage is "I'm going to kill him for what he did to me." Not only is rage larger than anger, but it is also tied in with retribution and revenge. With both emotions are accompanying feelings of helplessness and futility. At some level, you can't fix what is making you angry and full of rage.

Every spouse of a child molester I have interviewed and worked with has both feelings of rage and anger. For some women, they became the overriding feelings. For others, the feelings quickly melded into guilt and shame. But the anger and rage were always there, under the surface.

Abby always considered her husband the perfect father. He would bathe his children, tuck them in, and then say the Lord's Prayer before they went to sleep. Little did Abby know that he would slip his hands under the covers and molest them while they prayed together.

When she discovered he was molesting the children, Abby left him and sued for divorce and custody. He fought the custody suit, claiming she was an unfit mother. He was granted custody and she took the children into hiding rather than let him have them. Shortly after she left, her daughter became ill and was diagnosed with gonorrhea. Abby, believing that the diagnosis would support her allegations, again petitioned for custody. Her husband's attorney convinced the court that her three-year-old daughter had contracted the inflammation from a toilet seat. The custody order stood. The children were taken to their father's.

Abby finally gained custody of her daughter when her ex-husband was indicted on twenty-eight counts of child molesting, and he fled with the daughter. Her daughter, now a young teen, was six months pregnant by her father when she came back to her mother. Abby says now she would do anything to hide and protect a molested child, no matter what the judge said.

Going Crazy

Then you think you must be going crazy.

If you are experiencing such intense feelings, it is understandable you're having trouble thinking clearly, but it also takes a long time for the implications of the case to become evident and understood. You are getting new information that is highly emotionally charged. You may feel confused and uncertain. During this discovery time, it is not unusual for a woman to feel like she is going crazy: "I must be nuts," "This thing is too much for me," and "I'm feeling overwhelmed" are all common responses from women going through this phase of reaction. What is happening does not fit with what you know is true—not only about your personal experiences but what you expect from government systems, other people, and the way people should behave.

> *There was no question Jean's husband was molesting their daughter. She saw him do it. He said he was just changing his daughter's diaper, but the pediatrician verified that the baby had multiple internal scars and evidence of sexual abuse.*
>
> *Jean had thought their marriage was just fine. They had met in college, and even though he liked to party and she was the serious student, they quickly fell in love. His family was wealthy and well connected, so he had no problem finding a job when they got married. A new house, beautiful furniture, fancy vacations, it was all much more than Jean grew up with.*
>
> *Jean found out the other consequence of money and position when she filed for divorce and custody. The judge, a longtime friend of her husband's family, would not allow testimony on the allegations of molesting, insisting there was no substance to them. He granted Jean no support and gave custody to her husband, with minimal visitation to Jean. When she went back to court several months later, after again finding evidence of more abuse, the judge gave permanent full custody to her husband, with no visitation rights to Jean.*
>
> *The more Jean tried to work through the judicial system, the more frustrated she got. And the more the system fought back. She was eventually held in contempt of court and left the state, broke and disheartened. She not only felt betrayed by her husband, but by the judicial system as well.*

The very people she looked to for relief allowed their person-
al connections to the perpetrator's family to sabotage the
truth.

She was devastated. It felt like either she was crazy, that
she was so confused and upset by what she had gone through
that she no longer could tell what was truth and what was
reality, or that the American justice system was a sham, that
it was not the unbiased, impartial system she had believed it
was. Given those two alternatives, she started to question her
own sanity.

Several years later, the judge who had handled the
divorce and ensuing custody disputes retired. Jean received a
call from the court to come in and sign some papers. She
never officially found out why her case was reopened. The
new judge had reviewed her case, without her requesting it,
and reversed the previous findings. He granted Jean custody
of her children.

There is no one response pattern. There is no one right way to
respond. Some women choose to stay, believing their husbands and
disbelieving their children. For many women leaving presents a greater
challenge and more difficulties. They are faced with very expensive
legal bills, disbelief and blame from the courts, families, and friends,
and life alone. No matter what they do, they will be questioned, be disbelieved, be held accountable for their husbands' behavior, and have to
go through the hell of having their lives publicly examined by both
social services and the courts. Their children tend to blame them and
are angry no matter what they do. It is easy to see why they would feel
as victimized by their husbands' abuse as the children these men
harmed.

Being the spouse of a child molester is always there. When I
spoke with one woman, several years after the abuse was discovered
and after her children had grown, she said she still finds it difficult to
talk about the molestation, still keeps her secret, and still doesn't
understand why he continues to do what he does with other children.

Being the spouse of a child molester doesn't have to ruin your life completely, but it certainly colors it for the rest of your life. You may forgive, the volume may be turned down on your pain, but nothing can erase the experience.

Ambivalence

Trying to sort out your feelings is very hard. This is the man you loved, married, chose to have children with, committed to establish a life with. To find out something so horrifyingly awful about someone who you have been so close to and intimate with is almost unbearable. It is as if you have been sleeping with a stranger. Your spouse has kept from you the worst of secrets.

> Harvey had been in the military for nineteen years, and was close to retiring when Sheila discovered he was molesting their fifteen-year-old daughter. He was prosecuted, found guilty, and dishonorably discharged. He was sentenced to fifteen years in military prison.
>
> Because Harvey no longer receives his pay, Sheila must make good on their debts while supporting their children. She works two jobs, paying thousands of dollars in psychiatric bills for her daughter. In accordance with the military's rules and guidelines, her benefits stopped when his conviction was upheld. Sheila hates to admit it, but she continues to wonder if it might not have been better just to keep her mouth shut and not turn Harvey in. Even her friends' suggestions to get therapy to deal with her overt anger and frustration add to her pain. Not only does she have no time for therapy, she says, but even if she deals with her anger, she will still have the bills, her daughter will continue to be traumatized, and she will still be working two jobs.

If your options are limited, and you think "I have nowhere else to go" or "no way else to support myself or my children," the ambivalence is more acute. Then ambivalence carries over into difficulties with the logistics of living your life while in crisis. Questions of finances and administrative tasks escalate. In the face of these problems and issues, many women start to block out or even deny the abuse occurred. It is too painful to admit it happened. It seems easier to choose to stay.

SEXUALITY

Many women also report that they start to question their own sexuality and their own competence or adequacy as a woman.

> Beatrice can't understand why her husband did what he did. She says it might have made more sense if she had been absent, withdrawn, or unavailable, but she was none of those.
>
> When she was widowed at seventy, Beatrice looked back on a full life: she had fallen in love with her husband at twenty and loved him passionately until he died. He had been a successful and wealthy businessman, providing a very comfortable life for her and their three daughters. They had watched their children grow to adulthood, marry well, and start families of their own.
>
> Beatrice worried about her middle daughter, Barbara, who had accomplished many significant goals and enjoyed wide recognition, but always seemed anxious and unsettled. Finally, Barbara told Beatrice she was seeing a psychiatrist. The day after that conversation, Beatrice's husband had a fatal heart attack.
>
> Two months later, Beatrice's daughter revealed her father had sexually abused her from the time she was five until she left home for college at eighteen. At first, Beatrice couldn't believe it. She didn't think her daughter was lying, it was just that she couldn't imagine it. Her disbelief turned to distress when her younger daughter said it had happened with her also.

Wasn't I woman enough to make it not happen? is a common question many women ask themselves. Such a question ties into a spouse's sense of responsibility, guilt, and shame over her inability to provide total sexual satisfaction to her husband. A woman often believes her husband's sexuality is somehow her responsibility. If he acts out with his sexuality, it is because she is inadequate. In actuality, whether a person acts out sexually or not has more to do with himself, his wants, his needs, and his feelings than anything she has done or not done. And, as we've seen above, many molesters will try to blame anyone else rather than accepting responsibility for their own behavior. But the questions remain. Many women consider or have an affair to reassure themselves that their sexuality is intact and that they are sexually attractive and adequate.

Unfair Pain and Hurt

For many women, the underlying feeling they experience is a terrible sense of being wronged and of being treated unfairly. "He did something terrible and I'm the one who has to suffer." It is as if we were innocently driving down a road one day and a big truck came and ran over our lives.

In his book *Forgiving the Hurts We Don't Deserve*, theologian Lewis Smedes talks about unfair pain. He explains that when we are wronged by people we trusted to treat us right, we are not only hurt by their actions, but feel betrayed by their lack of consideration. We are hurt because they thought we deserved to be treated badly, they were doing it somehow for our own good, or they believed that they were being fair.

Even if people hurt us compulsively because they can't control themselves, or hurt us with the spillover from their own problems or when their good intentions go astray, it feels like betrayal. "If he really loved me, he wouldn't do this to me." "He did it and I suffer." It is difficult not to personalize the hurt.

When we are hurt by someone we have loved, we want that person to make amends, we want him to help with our healing. Child molesters not only don't help, they continue to deny they did anything or deny what they did was hurtful to anyone.

Waiting for our spouses to acknowledge their role in our pain hurts us more. When someone else causes an accident in which we are hurt and for which we need to heal, we can't wait for them to heal or to start healing us before we start our own recovery. We can't wait for them to accept the responsibility or to be found responsible for the accident. We need to get on with designing our own recovery process ourselves. Otherwise, like a broken leg that is not set properly, we risk it healing on its own and being crooked. When we delay taking care of ourselves, when we wait for the molester to admit he hurt us too, we delay our own healing. And like leaving a broken leg to heal by itself, we face the likelihood of being hurt more.

I kept trying to take care of and to heal everyone else. I tried to do what was best for my son, kept trying to fix my husband, and didn't take care of myself. Only when I gave up getting him to take responsibility for what he did and stopped trying to fix him, could I start fixing myself.

ISSUES

In addition to the initial reactions, often emotional and personal, there are several issues and logistical challenges that face every spouse of a child molester. More often than not, these are decisions that must be made, problems that need to be solved, and issues that involve the larger community. These issues revolve around questions of secrecy, who to tell what; feeling responsible and being blamed for what he did; and the isolation and lack of support from family, friends, and acquaintances.

Secrecy

Secrecy is the first issue. People like me, people like us, don't get involved with things like this. Child molesting is much too horrible to talk about. It is much too horrible to mention to anybody. The secrecy is based in both shame and guilt. To differentiate the two, shame is the belief that there is something inherently wrong with you; guilt is the belief you have done something wrong.

Shame is a judgment of one's sense of self, whereas guilt is a judgment based on one's behavior. When experiencing shame, who you are has been judged and found deficient. You have either judged yourself or been judged by others. Righteous people specialize in shame. They call on a higher authority, their religious beliefs, or common decency not only to label you as wrong or bad, but to back up their judgment. Righteous judgments are lethal because they hook very early shame messages. Most of us react to righteous judgments as if we were two years old. From this childlike perspective we believe only adults can talk. We act as children who are defenseless listeners who have to accept the adults' view as the truth of the world. Hooked into shame, it is very difficult to recover and respond. Rather, we wither under the attack and are not capable of defending ourselves.

Guilt, on the other hand, fueled by the belief you have done something wrong, gives rise to second-guessing and questioning: What have I done? What could I have done differently? Even though it was the husband or partner who was acting out, the experience is one of guilt by association. The next question becomes: What could I have done to have prevented the situation? What should I have done?

Twenty-Twenty Hindsight

Most of us live our lives looking forward and don't have the benefit of twenty-twenty hindsight. When we look back, we might clearly see signs that we missed when they were occurring. We then question how long we have been in denial, and why we weren't seeing the signs when they occurred.

> Neela was living with her sister and brother-in-law when he had been molesting neighborhood children. She reported later that there had been one or two incidents that had seemed strange at the time, like when she came home and found him and a child in the back bedroom, with the door closed. When he came out, with his hair wet and pulling his

clothes together, he explained they had been in the pool, and were changing. She said she had never dreamed that he could have been molesting the child. The thought had never even entered her mind. Now, she feels sad and guilty that she hadn't realized it, even while telling herself she couldn't have possibly known.

Feeling Responsible

We have been taught to be responsible for our own actions, and it is a quick step to feeling responsible for your spouse. You might be feeling like there was something you could have done that would have kept him in line. This type of "if only" conversation can be subtle, invasive, and surprising. "If only I had been more available," "If only I had been more understanding," "If only I had just been there." "If, if, if . . . if only I had done something differently, he would not have behaved the way he did." These conversations lead to feeling responsible for his behavior. Something you did, said, or were, caused it, made it, or let it happen.

Blamed for His Behavior

Many women also find it difficult to get help or understanding from friends and family. The response of friends and family is to inflict advice, discount the seriousness of the situation, or expect it to be resolved quickly. They act as if they know better than the woman involved what did happen, why it happened, and what she should do. It is not uncommon for them to try to take over and either imply or state outright the spouse of the molester is wrong, misperceiving, confused, or unknowing. The family of the perpetrator may deny that it could have happened at all. They are sure you must have been mistaken, that this was all a figment of your imagination. Others may trivialize the event by saying, "Well, yes, it did happen, but it was of little if any consequence." It is not uncommon for friends and family to blame the victim for enticing and/or seducing the molester into the behavior that he acted out. "If it hadn't been for the child, he wouldn't have done what he did. It is the child's fault."

The propensity of family and friends to give simplistic answers to extremely complex issues is probably the most difficult response to deal with. The complexity of the issues, the legalities, and the subtle nuances of a case often can tax the understanding of even the most intelligent, compassionate, and thoughtful. Upon hearing the frustration and the complaints of the spouse of a child molester, many friends insist that there is something that the woman can or could do now to make the situation different than what it is. They often insist that the courts or the police or the social service system just simply would not treat her the way she is claiming they did. This has the effect of denying to the woman what she is feeling and/or perceiving. The legalities and the actions of the social service/judicial system throughout the whole process are so incredibly complex that it is difficult, if not impossible, for someone who is not keeping up on a day-to-day basis to understand thoroughly the issues and the intricacies of the case at hand. Hearing parts of what is happening can lead family members and friends to unwarranted conclusions.

Sometimes friends and families fall victim to having little knowledge and make an armchair diagnosis. Several people insisted that I had obviously been abused myself as a child and that I was simply denying it. They would tell me that only someone who had been abused as a child would have married someone who turned out to be a child molester.

The other common response I dealt with was people insisting I must have known that it was happening, that it was impossible for me not to have known. In some ways I could understand how the social service system was making this accusation. They were strangers who didn't know me personally. It was difficult to deal with it when it was friends and family making the accusation. The very people I looked to for support and understanding didn't always give me the support I wanted. When I finally told one friend what was happening, she responded that she had known what he had been doing for a long time. Then she asked with disbelief how I could have missed it.

Isolation

Women often report feeling victimized by the "system," that is, the judicial social service, and victimized by the social workers who are supposed to be helping them, leaving them feeling extremely isolated. Even their paid professional helpers aren't sympathetic.

Because they don't know others in their situation, they feel as if no one else has ever gone through this, no one else has ever hurt like this.

Even if family and friends are supportive, they don't know or can't comprehend what's happening. Many women keep quiet for fear of alienating their friends, thinking they will tire of hearing about it. They feel they can't burden friends or family anymore with their story. This alienation grows to include most if not all of the people in their social/professional network.

Many women find it extremely difficult to talk about what they're feeling with their spouses, and to confront them with what is happening to both their lives. The reasons for not confronting the molesters vary with each case.

When I first heard the charges against my husband, I really believed they were not true. It didn't even dawn on me to ask him if they were true. I just knew they weren't. I knew we didn't have a perfect marriage, and had seriously considered divorce, but I didn't believe he could have done what he was accused of. Then, when I started to realize the charges could be true and told him so, he not only denied he did it, but told me I was crazy for believing others and not him. He continued to deny the charges until he died. At the same time, he continued not only molesting other children, but blaming me for abandoning him in his hour of need, calling my friends and family trying to get them to intervene and help me come to my senses, and insisting that I was un-Christian for not forgiving him and staying married to him. I stopped talking to him about it. No matter what I said he tried to turn it around so he was the victim and I was the persecutor. It became clear he and I did not see this issue the same way.

When the sexual abuse has been combined with verbal or physical abuse, many women do not confront the abuser for fear of their lives or the lives of their children.

If a custody or divorce case is underway, many women avoid talking with their spouses because anything they say can and will be used against them in court. Talking with the victims is also difficult, if not impossible. Feelings of guilt, for what could have been done to protect the child, are overwhelming. Talking with the victims' parents is usually not possible either. They are dealing with their own pain and anger. If the case is in litigation, your attorney may well suggest no contact between you and the other families involved. When the parents of the victims are people you have known for a long time, or have been friends or are family members, the loss is particularly difficult.

It is not uncommon for people to keep secret what has happened from their own families, including their parents, brothers and sisters, and other children. The sense of shame and fear of the consequences of making the situation public may be too much to risk.

Financial Issues
Financial issues loom very large. Not only are the fees for attorneys, therapists, and other professionals high, but it is not unusual to experience an inability to work and quite possibly a job loss. At the same time, everyday living expenses continue and may well increase with the need for additional baby-sitters and/or support help. For many families, just the cost of going back and forth to court and/or to attorneys and therapists becomes a considerable expense.

Professional Support
Dealing with the professional network of support is problematic at best. The clergy appears to have one of two reactions when a parishioner is accused of or arrested for molesting children. The members of the church may either become vindictive and unforgiving and want to punish the sinner, or embrace the sinner, bring him into the fold, and say that the church is the place where he can get the most help. In either event, the spouse of the molester is left out in the cold. When the perpetrator is approached to be punished by the clergy and the church, the spouse is often seen as part of the problem. (Some denominations excommunicate both the husband and the wife when the hus-

band has sinned sufficiently to be dropped from the fold. They believe her salvation is dependent upon his behavior.) When he is embraced by the church and brought into the fold, she is lost in the shuffle, seen as not needing help, or treated as the cause of the problem.

> *When Marie went to her pastor, he didn't believe her. Certainly her husband, the lead tenor in the choir, would never have done what she was accusing him of doing. Her husband kept singing each Sunday, and Marie finally left the church as the whispers and innuendoes increased. She never did confront her pastor about breaking her confidentiality. She said it was easier to leave the church she had grown up with than to face all her friends and their disbelief.*

Therapists have traditionally been unsympathetic and accusatory toward spouses of child molesters. As late as the mid 1970s, psychiatric textbooks were still attributing the major cause of male sexual acting out to the frigidity of the man's wife or sexual partner. Given this context, it is understandable that therapists are confused in terms of their treatment plan for somebody who finds herself in this situation.

> *Judy had been in treatment with several therapists when she came to a spouses-of-child-molesters support group. A registered nurse, she had been a supervisor in a busy surgical ward, was active in community theater, and contributed to the care of her ailing mother. One therapist had diagnosed her with inadequate personality, and paranoid ideation. She thought Judy was making up stories about her husband who was a pillar of the community, "to compensate for her own failings."*
>
> *A second therapist was sure this was a classic case of projection, based on her unresolved Oedipus/Electra complex issues, or in layperson terms, she really wanted to be a boy, envied male genitalia, and was accusing her husband of activities she wanted to do herself.*

The third therapist was the worst, Judy said. He diagnosed her as depressed and then prescribed so much medication, she found it hard to stay awake. When she asked him to cut back the medicine, he said he knew her family background. Depression ran in her family and she had been depressed for a long time and would always struggle with it. The medicine was the only way for her to feel better. He never would talk about what her husband had done. The problems was her depression not her husband's behavior.

Unfortunately, Judy's experience is not uncommon. The pattern of behaviors and feelings she was experiencing is typical of women who have lived with the ongoing stress of being married to a child molester. Yet, these normal and predictable responses are often classified as disorders, given a diagnostic label and number, and applied to the victim not the abuser. The victim is then treated as if she is mentally ill or neurotic rather than recognized as having a normally predictable reaction to an extremely traumatic event.

Departments of social services, judges, and lawyers represent another part of the helping professions that many spouses of child molesters find themselves unable or unwilling to get assistance from. Every woman who has gone through this experience has her own story of hell that her interaction with the social services system entailed. Oftentimes this floods over to include judges and lawyers as well.

My experience with the police investigating my husband for years, without ever approaching me, is typical. As is the officers telling me that the wife always sides with the husband. Conventional wisdom has it that women will not confront or turn in their abusing husbands. Yet that is not the case.

Judges and lawyers often see allegations of sexual abuse as attempts to manipulate the divorce or custody litigation. And, again, research has found this not to be the case.

MENTAL HEALTH DIAGNOSES

In addition to the emotional reactions and logistical issues all spouses of child molesters face, there are special considerations that occur when going for counseling or therapy. To understand the role of diagnosis, it is necessary to understand how third-party payments (insurance) and the mental health industry are interwoven.

All health insurance policies, health maintenance organizations, and government-provided health care plans have provisions for mental health care. Some may be very generous: paying for numerous outpatient visits, inpatient care, and/or medications. Others may be limited: paying for a specific number of visits, inpatient days, and specified medications. Still others may specifically exclude any conditions with a psychiatric diagnosis.

To submit any claim for payment, you must have a diagnosis. As unpleasant as that may be, you can't get reimbursement without one.

Lots of people have trouble with psychiatric diagnoses. There still is a stigma attached to being labeled "crazy" or "mentally ill." Some clients I have seen pay cash for therapy to avoid having a diagnosis. Some therapists only use the least noxious diagnosis (depression, anxiety, adjustment reaction) to avoid labeling their patients with a serious psychiatric condition. However you manage the system, you must have a diagnosis to get reimbursement.

Three diagnoses are commonly used for women who have been the spouse of a child molester: co-dependency, post-traumatic stress disorder, and depression. How they are experienced and how they are treated can make a lot of difference in a woman's being able to get on with her life and get beyond the stress and distress the experience has caused.

Co-Dependency

Spouses of child molesters often define themselves, or are defined by others, as co-dependent. Co-dependency is a concept that has blossomed incredibly in the last ten years, starting with Robin Norwood's book *Women Who Love Too Much*. Although an increasing number of books are being published every year on co-dependency, the number of self-defined co-dependents is increasing at a rate much higher than other types of addictions, particularly substance abuse addictions. If we can define co-dependency as an addiction, it is the most pervasive addiction.

At the same time there is still some confusion over the definition of co-dependency and what makes a person, especially a woman, co-dependent. There are some people who say that anyone who is in a significant relationship with someone who is addicted is co-dependent. Author Ann Wilson Schaef, in her book *When Society Becomes an Addict*, makes the point that there are so many co-dependent people that co-dependency is more of a description of our society than a personal problem.

While Robin Norwood did not use the word co-dependency in *Women Who Love Too Much*, the description she gave was consistent with later descriptions of behavior that is labeled co-dependent. The most common definition of co-dependency includes two factors:

- Seeing the source of your problems as outside of yourself, typically another person
- Attempting to control that other person's behavior

A co-dependent lets another person's behavior or feelings affect her to the point where she is no longer in charge of her own actions. She no longer acts on her own behalf, but reacts to other people. The second factor that is involved in co-dependency is control. The co-dependent person is obsessed with attempting to control the other person's behavior.

The types of situations and experiences that cause someone to become co-dependent are incredibly broad. They include people who are married to or living with a substance addict, people who have eating disorders, compulsive shoppers, gamblers, or sexual abusers. Anyone who works with, cares about, or loves people who are so addicted, or who has grown up in a family with one of these dysfunctions, is also considered by many professionals to be co-dependent.

One author made a case for co-dependency in a woman who grew up with deaf parents. Their deafness was the source of both family dysfunction and their daughter's co-dependency. As the only hearing person in the family, she was diagnosed as addicted to controlling their communication with the outside world! In fact, some professionals have gone so far as to suggest that well over 95 percent of the population of the United States today could be labeled co-dependent.

Characteristics of people who are co-dependent or who have been labeled codependent by others include:

- Caretaking
- Controlling
- Dependent
- Weak at setting boundaries
- Lacking trust
- Having sexual problems
- Shameful
- Guilt-ridden
- Questioning their own sexuality
- Ambivalent

and progressively getting worse in any and all of the above. Co-dependency is considered to be similar to other addictions and, like other addictions, is considered to be a disease. From a disease model of co-dependency, the condition is seen as progressive and powerful. The co-dependent will continue to get worse and worse, and there is little hope of curing the condition.

Using this model, it's easy to see how most women who are married to child molesters could be labeled by others as co-dependent, and probably feel co-dependent themselves. They are struggling to deal with a situation that most of them did not choose. At the same time, women who are married to child molesters feel the need to try to control their spouses' behavior, to stop the progression of shame, abuse, and disaster that is being brought into their lives. If you subscribe to the model of co-dependency, then there is no way to escape being labeled co-dependent. He has done something awful that is illegal and immoral and, as his wife, his actions have a direct impact on who you are, what kind of life you live, and what options are available to you.

In the co-dependency group that I was attending, other participants would confront me and say that I wasn't taking responsibility for what had happened. I couldn't blame him for the problems that I was experiencing. I was still trying to control him by making him responsible for our problems. And I had to stop seeing the source of my problems as outside of myself and start owning them. It became a catch-22 situation—I was being challenged to distance myself from his actions to determine what was his and what was mine. I had to get to the point where I could differentiate between what he was doing and my response to his actions. I had to establish boundaries between what was me and what was him. I had to stop trying to be responsible for him and start being responsible for me. And, at the same time, I had to deal with creditors and bankruptcy court, answer subpoenas, be a defendant in civil trials as his victims sued both of us, try to work, keep a roof over my head, and fulfill personal and professional obligations that had nothing to do with what happened.

Therapist Carol Travis makes the point that by looking at co-dependency simply as a personal response to dysfunction or difficulties within a relationship ignores the long historical tradition of women being treated as inadequate and socialized into positions of passivity and helplessness. We need to start to thinking of co-dependency not as a personal addiction but as a broader social problem. Her response to the label of co-dependency is to encourage women to look outward at the social, cultural, and environmental pressures they have experienced that have put them in a one-down position, rather than only assume they have to look inward to see what they have done wrong. It's the difference between being realistically angry at the subjugation of women and wanting that to change and looking inward and holding yourself responsible for everything that has happened, caused by your own inadequacies, shame, and guilt.

Both positions need to be acknowledged. Yes, you may not have always made the best choices. But, you did the best you could with who you were at the time, given the roles and lessons you were taught.

To get better, both the personal and the social issues need to be addressed.

Co-dependency treatment is a problematic concept for spouses of child molesters. If you join a twelve-step treatment program for co-dependency, you are quickly taught several lessons that may not be helpful to your own recovery. The first lesson is that your life is totally out of control and that you are addicted. Your addiction, co-dependency, is stronger than you are and there is no hope of recovery from it.

The second lesson you're taught is that you brought this all on yourself. The reason you're married to a child molester is you have done something wrong, there is something you need to fix, and he bears no responsibility for your pain and anguish. You chose to marry a child molester.

The third lesson is you will always be sick. Co-dependency is a disease from which there is no cure, no complete healing, and if you try to leave the group and/or make attempts to live a more competent lifestyle, other group members deride you for being in denial and use your attempts to live a more healthy life as evidence of how sick you are.

All of these lessons establish a very pessimistic outlook for making the necessary changes to take charge of your life.

I have several issues with co-dependency in general and especially applying it wholesale to spouses of child molesters. I do not subscribe to an illness model of co-dependency, but a model of learned, or socialized, behavior. Just as you have learned a pattern of behaviors and habits, you can learn new ones. This implies a hope and promise for changing, leaving ineffective behavior patterns behind you. You aren't doomed for life, you *can* get better. Your "illness" does not have to get worse.

I also see a dramatic difference between being married to someone who has a substance abuse problem and being married to someone who is a child molester. It is the difference between living with somebody who is addicted and someone who is evil. Whether you believe addiction is a disease or an uncontrolled habit, there is a hope that the addictive person will change. It is not unrealistic to expect things can and will get better when you change how you respond to your addicted loved one.

But, with child molesters, it is wishful thinking to believe he will change as you change. He is not going to change. Nothing you can do will ever make a difference in his abusive behavior. You didn't make him do it. You can't make him stop doing it. To hold yourself responsible for him and to expect you can make him change is absurd. And, it's co-dependent.

What makes it co-dependent is not that your troubles are coming from his illegal, immoral, evil behavior, but that your troubles are coming from your expectation that you can change him. As long as you hold to the belief that you can change him, you're never going to be free.

This is a very important and very subtle distinction. There is no denying that his behavior has totally disrupted and, in many ways feels like it has shattered, your life. You can recover from that. The greater challenge is letting go of the belief that somehow you can change him. You can't. He won't. And you'll just make it worse for yourself by continuing to try to do it.

Post-Traumatic Stress Disorder

Many, if not most, women exhibit symptoms of post-traumatic stress disorder (PTSD) in the weeks, months, and, sometimes even the years following the disclosure of their husbands' abuse and the resulting legal and emotional hassles. Although PTSD was first described in reference to combat victims and victims of natural disasters, there are numerous parallels with postabusive disclosure.

PTSD is a label that is used to refer to a collection of symptoms that people experience following a psychologically stressing event that is outside the range of the usual human experience. Typically, the distressing event is much longer lasting and more severe when the stressor is of human design, such as abuse or war, than when it is a natural disorder. Each person experiences her own unique collection of symptoms, which may or may not be shared by others who have had similar types of trauma. Most often the stressing event is persistently re-experienced either by intrusive thoughts or recurring dreams called flashbacks. Flashbacks may be so real that it is hard to believe that the trauma isn't happening again. A flashback can last for minutes or even hours. Often the anniversary of the event, similar events, or similar places trigger flashbacks.

People with PTSD often report shutting down their emotions. They feel detached, unable to think clearly, uninterested in the activities they previously enjoyed. Many people report little interest in sex and withdraw from friends and family.

Hypervigilance, or being unusually alert and restless, is also common. Difficulty in falling or staying asleep is common as well as being irritable and upset about minor annoyances. Often people have trouble concentrating or are unusually sensitive to being startled. It is as if they are waiting and watching for the next bad thing to happen.

Unless dealt with, PTSD can become chronic, manifesting in symptoms of anxiety, depression, sleep disorders, and impaired relationships. Self-medication is common with advertised or unadvertised mood-altering substances, either over-the-counter medications or alcohol. As a result it may be necessary to deal with substance abuse along with the PTSD.

Unless there are severe symptoms of self-destructive behavior that would necessitate intensive one-on-one therapy or hospitalization, group therapy is the treatment of choice for PTSD. However, because of intense feelings of withdrawal, or shame and guilt, participating in group therapy may be problematical. Nonetheless, it works better and faster, and can be of more help sooner than other treatment methods, enabling the woman to feel better faster.

Depression

One of the most common and predictable responses of women who have learned to be helpless in the face of a difficult, if not impossible, situation is depression. When it comes to depression, the most potent consequences on spouses of child molesters is the inability to take action and overwhelming lethargy. It is difficult to think about leaving someone or getting on with your life when you are in the throws of depression. If you find that you want to take to your bed, haven't showered or gotten dressed for several days, or cry all the time, suspect depression and ask for help. Until you address your depression, it will be hard to do anything for yourself.

Being depressed, or experiencing depression, does not mean you are crazy, a sinner, or mentally incompetent. Depression is a mood disorder that can range from moderate to severe, lasting a short time or a lifetime. Some depressions are responsive to medications, others responsive to therapy, others are intractable, meaning nothing is able to help.

The major myth associated with depression is that "it is all in your head." While it is true that keeping active often helps, depression needs medical and/or psychological treatment. It is not a condition that responds effectively to avoidance and waiting for it to go away by itself.

The symptoms associated with depression can be moderate to severe, and may well range in severity over time. Some of the symptoms are reflected in mood: irritability, crying easily, loss of joy and satisfaction in what you do and your life, feelings of hopelessness and helplessness, and most especially a feeling of lethargy, or not wanting to do anything but sit around and feel awful. Somatic symptoms are also common: wanting to sleep all the time, not being able to sleep, falling asleep without trouble but waking up in the early hours of the morning and not being able to get back to sleep. Some people report insatiable hunger. Others say nothing appeals to them and they just can't bring themselves to eat. Headaches, stomachaches, digestive troubles with constipation or diarrhea, trouble breathing, racing heartbeats, may be typical for people with depression.

Thinking distortions are also common. People who are depressed always see the glass as half-empty. They notice the negatives in any situation, while missing the positives. They get into all or none thinking, where one small flaw will discount the rest of their perfect performance. They catastrophize, always expect the worst, quickly jump to negative conclusions with little evidence. They "should" themselves unmercifully, expecting perfection and then judging their flaws severely. They are also convinced their negative view of themselves, their situation, and their lives is the truth. Anyone who sees things differently, or more optimistically, is wrong at least, deluded at worst.

Depression is labeled either reactive or endogenous. Reactive depression is the result of a loss or traumatic event. The depressed person is reacting to what has happened with depression. Endogenous depression comes from within. It is not associated with a specific event or situation but seems to come from how a person interacts with her own life.

There is a real difference between being depressed and being sad. Usually sadness comes from loss, the loss of a loved one, the loss of an opportunity, or the loss of a dream. We respond to the loss with feelings of sadness and grief that eventually are resolved over time. While you may still feel the loss, you readjust your life and find a new way of making a life for yourself.

Reactive depression may be thought of as being sad about being sad. Rather than resolving the issues of loss, you continue to feel the loss every day and dwell on what is lost rather than getting on with making a new life.

If you are treated for depression, the treatment you receive will depend on what theory of depression your therapist subscribes to. Cognitive therapy has been found to be the most effective in dealing with depression. It teaches you new ways to combat depressing situations so that you can armor yourself against recurrent episodes. *The New Mood Therapy* by therapist David Burns is an excellent book about depression and cognitive therapy. He explains clearly what depression is and includes many exercises and activities to help you feel better.

Many more women than men experience depression. This is not surprising, given the socialization patterns and pressures many women face. It would be surprising to find you weren't feeling at least sad, if not depressed, when you discover that your husband is a child molester. It *is* sad, and even depressing. Be careful though, that you don't let yourself slip over into a full-blown depression.

Medication is always problematic when it comes to depression. I kept thinking that I didn't want to take medication, I didn't want to admit I was as depressed as I was, surely I could pull myself out of this. I was going to a therapist, surely I would start to feel better soon.

Finally, I asked my therapist if he could give me a little something. He smiled and said he had been waiting for me to ask for it. He knew if he suggested it I would have rejected it out of hand. It had to be my idea, and I had to get to a point of no return before I asked.

I have taken numerous other medications over the course of my life, but never have I had such a hard time becoming accustomed to taking this little pill. I forgot to take it, I lost a bottle of pills in my own kitchen. I couldn't remember if I had taken a pill. I did everything I could to mess up the medication. I just didn't want to take it. Finally, I got into a routine and accepted the fact that I had to have some psychopharmaceutical help.

Psychotropic medication is not like antibiotics or painkillers. You don't feel the effects within hours or a day after taking them. It can take weeks to start to feel the effects. And when you do, the effects may be subtle at first. You feel like the edges are smoothed over, and everything isn't so rough.

Medication will not solve your problems, but it will help you feel better so you can take care of them yourself. Medication is not a substitute for therapy nor is it a permanent way to escape or deny the issues that started you feeling bad in the first place. Most physicians will be as conservative as they can, giving you the lowest possible dosage to alleviate your symptoms, for the shortest time necessary so you can take care of your problems. And, get on with your life.

TREATMENT GROUPS

In my experience with groups for spouses and partners of child molesters, I found that the group process, sharing the feelings and knowing that you are not alone, is in and of itself incredibly healing for the participants. Often, the women in the groups had never shared with anyone else how they felt about being spouses of child molesters. Many had never talked to other women who have shared their experience.

It is important to differentiate between mother's groups and spouse's groups. In mother's groups, participants deal with their feelings of not having interfered and protected their children more quickly. They deal with being the recipient of their children's anger and frustrations and, most commonly, struggle with their own feelings of guilt. In groups for spouses of child molesters, the topics include dealing with the shame and sense of responsibility for their spouse's behavior, but also, and most importantly, dealing with the spouse's own anger that her husband did such terrible things and that because of his behavior her life has been permanently altered. Most women in these groups report that "Plan A" for their lives was not to marry someone who would be a child molester, and having to pick up the pieces afterward is extremely stressful.

Many women attend both a mother's group and a spouse's group, reporting there are very different sets of issues they are dealing with and healing over in each group.

Chapter 5

So Why Don't They Leave?

*If we do not know our own history, we are doomed to live
it as though it were our private fate.*
— HANNAH ARENDT, German-American philosopher

Little if any systematic research has been conducted on why spouses of child molesters stay in the abusive situation. Each player in the drama has her own reason why she stays or leaves. And whether she stays or leaves, she can be sure there will be plenty of people who will criticize her and find fault with the decision she made.

One social service supervisor dismissed the question, saying that the spouses of child molesters were sicker and crazier than their molesting spouses. He angrily claimed that the women should be locked up, that they were the real perpetrators. When I pressed him for the reasons for his viewpoint, he would only say that they should have taken action. It is their responsibility to stop their spouses. It became clear that this issue had become personal and emotional for him. He had lost his professional perspective on spouses of child molesters, including them with the molesters themselves as perpetrators rather than including them as victims of the molesters with the children who were abused.

Yet, his view reflects that of many people who see child molestation as the wife's responsibility to manage her husband's sexual behavior. She is expected to be in control of her family, both her children and her husband.

Academicians and clinicians have examined the motives and reasoning of women who stay and women who leave. Parallels have been drawn with women who have been physically abused or battered, and the reasons they give for staying or leaving. (Appropriately so, for about half of the women who are physically abused are also sexually abused by their batterers.) Gender socialization theorists look to what women and men have learned to be as an explanation of why women stay in a marriage with a molesting spouse. Research on animals who learned to be helpless has been extended to women who have endured long-term trauma in their marriages. There are many suggestions of reasons why women stay or leave. There are no sure answers.

Again, the theories and suggested causes vary. There is no one answer. As you read through the following be sure you monitor your own reactions and pay attention to which approaches you agree with or disagree with. Like deciding how much and what a woman knows about the abuse, where and why she stays or leaves generates very strong feelings. For spouses of child molesters, it is one more instance of being caught in a no-win situation. Whatever she decides, there will be many angry, hostile critics to tell her she is wrong and has made her situation, the children's experience, and even the consequences for her molesting spouse, worse.

Typically, women who aren't battered or women who aren't in an abusive situation, when hearing about a woman who is, proclaim loudly they would never let anyone do that to them. Certainly, they say, she does have choices and why doesn't she "just leave."

In response to this reaction, several points are worth mentioning:

- Behavior that is rewarded is more apt to be repeated. This is one of the classic "rules" of psychology. When you are rewarded for acting a particular way, you'll do it again. The sticking point here is what is rewarding. Rewards can be positive: a smile, a hug, attention, praise, money.

Rewards can also be the cessation of negative actions: stopping getting hit, stopping being yelled at, or being given the silent treatment. Rewards shape our behavior. When rewards are not given, or if the behavior tends to drop out over time, we react to these patterns.

- Being able to decide to take action or not to take action gives a certain amount of control over a person's life.

We develop patterns of behavior in our relationships. Like a ballet we have choreographed and practiced, we know who does what and when. I expect the dance to be the same each time.

Then the day comes when the dance isn't the same. I step forward, expecting you to step back—and you don't. So, I try stepping right—expecting you to step right too. And you step left, or forward, or back. The dance pattern continues to break down: no longer is our dance predictable. No longer can I expect my behavior to have a predictable effect on your behavior. No longer am I a partner in our dance. I begin to learn that it doesn't matter what I do, you will dance your own dance. Pretty soon, I stop dancing. If you don't see a connection between what you do and the response you get from others, pretty soon you stop trying to do anything. You learn to passively accept whatever comes your way. You stop believing you have control over what happens to you.

Once we believe we cannot control what happens to us, it is difficult to believe that we can ever influence it, even if later we experience favorable outcomes.

Gender Socialization

Gender socialization refers to the early lessons we all learn about how to be men and women, and how to relate to one another. The typical socialization pattern that many children learn is that males are active, strong, and in charge. Females are often seen as less capable, passive, and followers. Although this is changing somewhat as girls increasingly have positive role models, there is still a long way to go. Many sociologists suggest that the gender socialization many women experienced as young children leaves them vulnerable to becoming victims of men who are socialized into abusive behavior. In other words, many women learn early on that what men do to them is something over which women have little, if any, control. And once in a situation, once they have "made their bed," they have no other choice but to lie in it.

Tina watched her father beat her mother. He would hit her and call her names, especially when he was drunk. Tina's mother was terrified of her husband, and terrified he would hit the kids. She "took it" from him to protect the children. She stayed because she had no education, no training, no money, and no one else who could support her. She had "learned" there was nothing else she could do.

   Tina learned the lesson too. Her husband started by taking her paychecks, and began to whip her because she deserved it, he claimed, for not keeping the house and their four children spotless in addition to not making enough money.

Watching her parents, Tina learned that husbands beat their wives and terrorize their children. Tina's marriage was just what her parents had taught her marriage was, and should be. Her husband had learned his lessons well also. He learned it was okay to hit his wife, take all the money, and "be the boss."

Social learning theory holds that the perception of control over events in a woman's life contributes to the way she feels about herself and her ability to take action. If she perceives she has no control, she will act as if she has none.

Tina firmly believed that her childhood experiences modeled how "marriage" is for everyone. She didn't see she had any other choice but to stay with her husband. She was sure she had no control over her life. When other women tried to tell her there were things she could do, she would only say maybe they could, but she certainly couldn't.

LEARNED HELPLESSNESS

The concept of learned helplessness is often used to explain the passivity and ambivalence of battered women. It can also be useful in understanding why some women choose to stay with a molester.

The passivity battered women demonstrate and their inability to leave an abusive situation, even when they are shown the way out, was found to be strikingly similar to the behavior of animals who had learned to be helpless. In this study, the researchers had not intended to teach the animals to be helpless. But, when they were investigating another behavior, some of the animals were subjected to random abuse, from which they could not escape. They reacted to this trauma by becoming very passive. In his work with these animals, psychologist Martin Seligman found the animals had lost their ability to act in their own best interests. They stopped trying to escape the abuse, and passively accepted whatever was done to them. Even when they were shown a way out, they seemed unable to learn new behaviors to help themselves. They stayed in the painful situation.

This combination of not being able to escape and the randomness of the abuse quickly reduced the animals to a condition called "learned helplessness." They would passively accept the abuse and appear to wait for the next incident to occur. Since they had learned there was nothing they could do to control or stop the abuse, they did nothing. And they were unable to accept a more adaptive response. Even when shown a way out they wouldn't take it. They were unable to learn new patterns of behavior that were self-enhancing.

These behavior patterns are similar to what most women who are abused have learned. They are subjected to random abuse, over which they have no control. And, they are sure there is no escape. Whether because they are unskilled and can't work to support themselves and their children, fear he will hurt them worse for trying to leave, or have no where to go, they see no escape as possible. And like the animals who had been abused, even when shown a way out, they can't take action.

Researchers found the animals who learned to be helpless would accept abuse rather than take an escape that was clearly offered. When you learn to be helpless, you have trouble believing your actions will make a difference. You get stuck in helplessness.

Learned helplessness results in apparent disturbances in both emotional and physical well-being. Depression and anxiety are common, as are psychosomatic disorders: sleeplessness, irritability, difficulties with eating and/or elimination.

It is extremely difficult to get beyond learned helplessness. Even when encouraged, shown role models who have been successful, given information about alternatives, and "shown the way out," most women who have learned to be helpless have trouble taking charge of their lives. They get stuck in their helplessness. Their view of themselves as helpless is more potent than the reality of their choices. To change, to become more proactive, and to take charge of their lives is very difficult. That some women are able to take this step is testimony to their courage and hard work.

DEPRESSION

As a part of learned helplessness, post-traumatic stress disorder, and the predictable consequence of learning your spouse is a child molester, depression and the accompanying lethargy are also factors in why many women stay in their marriages. It is just too difficult to face the logistical and emotional trauma of having to find a new place to live, take the children into new schools, and face the financial trauma of moving. The logistical issues alone are overwhelming for someone who is in the throes of depression. Even if she can consider the possibility of leaving, getting the energy together to do it is extremely difficult.

COLLUSION

Collusion is often involved in the dynamics of deciding to stay or to leave. Collusion is a secret agreement to hide the reasons behind your behavior. It can be a very potent determining factor in how you make your decisions and what you choose to do. Collusion is a nonconscious process. You don't talk about acting or overtly agree to act in a particular way, but you consistently do. You can hide from outsiders or even from yourself, the *real reasons* for your actions, and attribute your motivation to *good reasons.*

> *Lenore was furious when her sister, Jane, and niece, Nancy,*
> *confronted Lenore about her husband's behavior. As a new*
> *young mother, Nancy was very uncomfortable about letting*
> *her uncle hold or touch her baby daughter. She began to*
> *remember how he had touched and held her when she was a*
> *child. She confided in her mother and then the two of them*
> *went to Lenore. Lenore would not listen to their concerns, and*
> *steadfastly refused to believe their allegations. She said they*
> *were just envious of her more prosperous life and told them*
> *never to come back to her house. She would not let them*
> *speak to her husband and threatened that if they ever thought*
> *of going public with their accusations she would retaliate.*

Lenore and her husband have an unspoken agreement: they collude to hide his secrets. She shields him from the accusations and bullies the accusers to be silent. She chooses to stand by her man, rather than listen to her sister's accusations. Lenore goes along with her husband's behavior because she is getting something from staying with him. She is colluding with him because she is getting a payoff too. Sometimes the payoffs from collusion are trivial and inconsequential, other times they are significant and destructive.

Typically, when you get caught up in collusion, you have little awareness of your part in the process. If her sister had confronted Lenore with her role in the abuse, Lenore would have replied she was doing what she should have been doing: standing by her husband when he was attacked by family members. The insidiousness of collusion is that you usually don't realize that you have made a choice, or that there are even other choices available.

MASOCHISM

The myth that women stay in abusive relationships because they want to be or enjoy being abused needs to be addressed here also. Based on a model of female masochism, the notion of enjoying abuse depends on believing women get pleasure from pain, and that women are appropriate targets for abuse. This view is used to support the abusers' belief that women somehow ask for abusive treatment and thus their abusive behavior is warranted. Although the reasons women give for having stayed as long as they did may be different after they leave, seldom, if ever, do you hear women say that they stayed in the relationship because they enjoyed being beaten.

LOGISTICAL ISSUES

The reasons why women have difficulty leaving abusive relationships form an incredibly complex psychosocial framework. Many times there are economic, legal, and social dependencies that preclude her leaving. If a woman has been a homemaker and has not worked for a number of years, has small children, or has no money of her own, it is very difficult for her to see that she is going to be able to support her family without the man as the breadwinner.

Particularly when sexual abuse is part of a general pattern of abuse, the fear of being hurt more for leaving is a factor. Often women report they are afraid to leave because there is no safe place to go. They know their spouses will be angry enough that they will follow and attempt to hurt them or the children if they do leave. Unfortunately, this is true often enough that it cannot be discounted as a reason for staying. Social service agencies and even the police do not offer adequate protection to women who are attempting to leave abusive situations.

Unwittingly, psychologists, marriage counselors, family therapists, and pastors may counsel the woman to keep the family together at any cost. It is more important for the children to be in an intact home and an intact family than to disrupt their lives—even if the home environment is angry and threatening.

> *Diandra finally got the nerve to approach her physician, asking his advice on what she should do about her marriage.*
> *Her husband was consistently emotionally abusive and she discovered that he was sexually acting out. Too embarrassed*

*to tell the physician that her husband was molesting her
daughter, she said he was having sexual relations with someone else. The physician smiled, winked, nudged her a bit,
and said, "Well, men will be men. They all do that and a
part of your responsibility as a good wife is to stay with him.
It's no big thing."*

Probably the most important logistical factor in the issue of
women who stay in abusive relationships is their fear that they cannot
survive alone. Whether the survival is seen in an emotional, financial,
or legal framework, women are afraid that they can't do it by themselves without a man in the household. Even when they are assured
that they can survive financially, the prospect of being a single parent
with a number of small children is so daunting that they choose to put
up with a bad marriage rather than face the pressures of trying to go it
alone.

Next Steps

Finding out you are the spouse of a child molester changes your life
forever. Whether you are in the early days of discovering the betrayal
and the pain he has caused, or dealing with his ongoing abuse and the
possibility of physical abuse of you as well as the children, the pain is
exquisite. When you are in throes of the early pain, it is impossible to
believe that your life will ever be the same, or that the pain will ever
stop.

I kept waiting for the other shoe to drop, not knowing when I
would hear about another child who was coming forward with an accusation, or another friend or family member who had realized he or she
had witnessed an incident and hadn't understood at the time what was
happening. I couldn't sleep, I was afraid to answer the phone, I was
afraid of what I would learn next.

If someone had told me then that I would not only stop being
afraid, but that I could put my life back together and heal myself and
my child, I would not have believed them. And yet, I did. It wasn't easy,
and it took a long time. I had the help of friends, family, and even

strangers in my journey of healing. I was also hampered by friends, family, and even strangers on that journey. I learned a lot, changed a lot, and did things I never thought someone like me would do. I made mistakes, took wrong turns, and made some dumb decisions along the way. I am older, wiser, and a different person today than I was on that day that the phone rang and my husband told me of his arrest.

My new beginning came on a November morning when I finally realized that no matter what I did, there was no way I could change what he had done, or would continue to do. I couldn't make him change, or even accept responsibility for what he did. I had to stop taking care of him and start taking care of myself. I finally told myself the truth about him and me and what I needed to do. Telling myself the truth was the important first step in turning my life around.

There were other things I needed to do: reclaim my power, stop letting others define my life and define it myself. I had to start standing up for myself better, being more assertive, being more aggressive at making decisions, looking at the problems I had and using what I knew to solve and resolve some of them so I could get on with my life. I didn't know it that day, but I had to come to some sense of forgiveness . . . for what he did to me, not for being who he was, and not for what he did to the children. They would have to forgive him for what he had done to them. I didn't know then that it isn't possible to forgive someone for who he is.

But, most importantly, I had to take action. When I designed the treatment program for myself, I was making a commitment to take care of myself, to do for me what I knew so well to do for others. It had come time for me to mother mama . . . and to get on with my life.

The second part of this book is the story of that journey. I was privileged to share the journey with a number of other courageous women, women who had found themselves in the same position I had. They said they had never talked with anyone else who had been through what they had been through. The individual therapy sessions and support groups I conducted became healing experiences for all of us. This book would not have been possible if they had not been willing to share their pain and deal with it so openly.

Part II

Taking Action

Chapter 6

Facing the Truth

If you don't know you know, you think you don't know.
— R. D. LAING, British psychologist

When first faced with the knowledge and realization of their husbands being child molesters, most women react with feelings of anger, betrayal, disbelief, and shock. One woman replied that all she could keep saying to herself was, "This couldn't be happening . . . this couldn't be happening." Another woman confided that she kept feeling like she was in a bad dream. When I sat in the attorney's office the day my husband was arrested, I can remember the attorney saying, "You'll experience one hundred days of hell." As it turned out, the hundred days stretched out to almost a thousand days, and my feelings of numbness, shock, and anger engulfed me most of those days.

Wanting to start a recovery program is not something that most women think of first. Many women have a hard time believing their lives will ever have meaning again. While it is true that your life will never be the same, it does not need to be true that your life is ruined.

Being able to take the initial steps from shock and grief to putting your life back together is a formidable task. For many of us it seems like we will be stuck forever in shock and grief. However, the maxim that time heals, while a trite cliché and hard to believe when you're going through the pain, holds true. Being able to recover, moving off from initial pain, shock, and grief, and getting on with your life depends in large part on telling yourself the truth: that is, acknowledging what has happened and how bad you feel. Motivational speakers, ministers, and school teachers tell us we have to know where we're starting from before beginning our journey. Telling yourself the truth is the important first step in your journey to reclaim your life.

TIME TO HURT

In his book *Transitions*, therapist Bill Bridges suggests that every crisis or major life change we experience starts with an ending rather than a beginning. The way we have become accustomed to living changes because something has ended. The ending can be a crisis: an accident with serious injuries or death, the loss of a job, divorce. Spouses of child molesters face the grim reality that the life they thought they were living is not, in fact, what has been happening all along.

> *Vanessa described her wedding day as the "happiest day of her life." A nurse, she was marrying a young physician whose life held a great deal of hope and promise. She was longing to establish not just a marriage but also the beginnings of a family. She wanted to fill the gap that she experienced when her mother died when she was a young child. Her father struggled to raise her younger sister, Cindy, and herself with little if any help from the larger extended family. When her father died when Vanessa was in high school, she became mother and father to her younger sister. Although they stayed with their grandmother, Vanessa was Cindy's primary caretaker. But Vanessa still longed for a home of her own, and a husband and babies to fill it up.*
>
> *The dream that she had was not to happen. Cindy was only thirteen when Vanessa got married. Soon after the wedding, Cindy became uncharacteristically distant and didn't*

want to spend time with Vanessa and her new husband. Finally, some eight months after the wedding, Cindy confided that her new brother-in-law had forced her to have intercourse with him the morning of the wedding.

For Vanessa, what ended for her was her dream of having a happy and family-oriented life with her new husband. For many women who are married to child molesters, the crisis that they experience, the ending of life as usual, comes not as a result of their own behavior, but as a result of someone else's behavior. Yet their lives are inextricably bound to that crisis.

After the ending and before the beginning is a period of time that Bridges calls the neutral zone. During this neutral zone there is a feeling of hopelessness, despair, and having your life placed on hold. Some people describe this time as a black hole or a swamp. The pain and anger are unrelenting and intense.

One woman described it as feeling like a cat who needed to go off in the corner to lick her wounds. She was unable to deal with anything and simply wanted not to address any of the issues, any of the hurts, any of the pain that she was experiencing. She just wanted to sit and wait for it to go away.

It is while in this neutral zone that well-meaning friends and family members may encourage you to pull yourself together, to get on with your life, to deny or minimize the experiences that you've had, and to discount your need to allow yourself hurting and healing time. Resist their suggestions. You need to validate and honor your feelings of pain or hurt, not deny them.

If you try to hurry and start to take action before you are ready, or before you are finished hurting, you'll find that your efforts will come to naught. It may well be that friends and family, watching you go through your pain, are in as much pain as you are and simply want you to feel better so that they don't have to feel so bad. Nonetheless, you can't hurry your healing process just to help them feel better.

Bridges talks about the neutral zone not as something to be gotten through as quickly as possible but as a time to really think things over and evaluate what has occurred. You need to take time to work through the important inner business of transition. Although your outward behavior may appear aimless and disconnected, important work is going on in the inside.

Beginnings are more subtle and often are difficult to pinpoint. Unlike the crisis that marks the start of a transition period, new beginnings are characterized by subtle shifts and changes, tentative first steps, and very small and even trivial new behavior. Only by looking back is it possible to acknowledge the new beginning.

There is the urge to start a new beginning arbitrarily and artificially by declaring a time to "get on with it." So you choose a day to stop feeling bad and to start to get on with life. Typically, what happens is the day comes and goes, you take a few steps, but they are quickly lost in the shuffle of re-experiencing and reviewing the pain and anguish you have been dealing with.

Face Your Feelings

One of the most important steps to take during that neutral zone, and before the new beginning starts, is to face your feelings. I've often had clients who come into therapy and relate a story of a difficult, anguished experience they've had. They tell how bad they're feeling. Then they judge themselves. They feel bad about feeling bad. It is as if they have guilt or shame about feeling angry, upset, or frustrated over having had a bad experience.

Feeling bad is what you're supposed to feel when bad things happen.

Feeling bad about feeling bad not only serves no purpose at all but it gets in the way of dealing with your pain and resolving the situation. It is important not to judge either yourself or your feelings as being unpleasant, inappropriate, or shameful.

One of the hardest feelings to face, or even to admit to, is a feeling of murderous rage. Most spouses of child molesters share in an unguarded moment they wish their husbands were dead. Some of them wish that they could kill them themselves. For most of us, homicide is not an attractive option. Seeing ourselves as homicidal maniacs is not attractive. Nonetheless, most of us have felt that way when we finally realized what our spouses have been doing.

I have participated in support groups or in therapy sessions where women have found their feelings range from homicide to suicide, depression to anxiety, hysterical glee at images of bloody revenge to primitive wailing of grief and pain. Feelings are what you feel. Judging them and seeing yourself as bad for having them only gets in the way of the healing process.

Not attending to your feelings, denying them, or minimizing what you're feeling delays your healing process. Stuffing your feelings with depression is not only ineffective but can hinder your recovery process.

Sometimes friends and family either try to tell you how to best handle your feelings, or suggest what you're going through is no big deal. They minimize your experience of your pain. They may tell you that you aren't *really* a victim and you should count your lucky stars, pull yourself together, and just get on with this. By denying either the importance or the impact of what is happening, you'll again keep yourself stuck and not get on with your healing.

Sometimes women attempt to diminish or deny their feelings because they are afraid their feelings will take over. They're afraid that if they feel strongly or experience fully the feeling they have, they'll be unable to control their behavior and their thoughts.

Let's make a clear distinction between feeling deeply, thinking clearly, and acting purposefully. Just because you have homicidal, maniacal thoughts about what you would like to do to the man who has victimized you as well as the children doesn't mean that you're going to act on them.

Alice reported that she had ongoing dreams, even daydreams, about wanting her husband dead and/or maimed. She was so angry and so hurt that she wanted him to hurt in the same way. When one of her friends asked her why she just didn't shoot him and get it over with, she drew herself up, thought for a moment, and then replied with all seriousness, "He isn't worth spending the rest of my life in jail."

Alice made a clear distinction between what she was willing to think about and what she was willing to do. She knew that she was deeply hurt. She knew that she had bloody, vengeful thoughts. And, she knew that she could control her behavior. Unlike her husband, who seemed unable to control his behavior, she could recognize the consequences of doing what she was thinking about. She could choose actions that were in her best interest.

When the newspapers printed stories of my husband's activities, I received several phone calls from both acquaintances and strangers saying they could take care of "things" for me. It took awhile for me to realize what the callers were offering. And for cheap. Several just wanted expenses, others no more than one thousand dollars. I would be lying if I told you I didn't consider taking one of them up on the offer, particularly the fellow who offered to make it look like an accident.

It is important, too, to honor your *own* feelings and reactions. It is common to believe anyone would feel like we do, that universal feelings are somehow connected to the event that occurs. But, feelings arise from our reactions to these events, not to the events themselves. It is not uncommon for different people to have very different and distinct reactions to the same situation. While we might be able to understand another person's thoughts, feelings, and actions, it does not necessarily mean that they will be or should be the same as ours.

Ellie Nessler, a California mother of a young boy, was convicted of killing the man who had been molesting her son. She reported that when she entered the small courtroom where the man was on trial, his sneering at her and his seductive glances at her son caused something to snap inside of her. She drew a gun from her pocket and shot him dead.

In a support group for spouses of child molesters, shortly after the incident occurred, virtually every woman could understand and appreciate how she had felt, wanting to kill the man that had hurt her son so badly. However, a number of the women in the group said that they would never shoot anyone, had never handled a gun, or would have chickened out had they been faced with the same option.

One of the most difficult issues to face is your initial denial of what has actually occurred. At first, most spouses of child molesters, myself included, don't believe the charges against their husbands. Then later, when it becomes evident the charges are true, they feel guilty and shameful for not recognizing the truth of the charges right away. These guilty feelings can be very difficult to deal with, especially if in your initial reaction you believed your husband and disbelieved the child who was abused. Your pain can be compounded if social workers, therapists, or attorneys accuse you of "being in denial" and thus contributing to or causing the abuse.

Denial is an automatic human response to a difficult or horrific situation. It is accompanied by being overwhelmed and/or not knowing how to react, feeling immobilized. When we are faced with difficult and serious changes, most of us don't want to accept that a change is happening. For most of us, when we hear something awful has happened, the first words out of our mouths are "Oh no" or "It couldn't be." We spend a fair amount of time pretending nothing has happened. Or, for a few moments when we first wake up in the morning, we forget things have changed, and think, or maybe wish, our lives are just the way they used to be. Sometimes the denial is so profound we may seem to be in a state of suspended animation, living life day to day, going through the motions without feeling the pain. This numbing response to stress is typical and, fortunately, usually short lived.

Depression and Guilt

When the denial and dismay deepen, depression is likely. Depression and guilt are the low points in the reaction process. Worry and anxiety about what the change will bring, an acute sense of loss, and personal powerlessness increase the feelings of depression. This can be a time of great guilt, because you could have, or should have, or might have, done something that would have made a change in the situation. "If only" is a favorite phrase that is used during this time. "If only" I had been more careful, "if only" I had been different, then he wouldn't have done what he did. The distorted thinking here is that you believe his behavior was dependent upon who and what you are rather than who and what he is. Some people get so stuck in depression and guilt that they literally spend the rest of their lives feeling bad for a situation over which they may have had little, if any, control. Others move on to the next step.

ACCEPTANCE AND COPING

Acceptance and coping characterize the turning point in recovery. Acceptance and coping imply that there is a recognition your life has changed and that it's not going to ever be the same again. It doesn't mean that you have to like the change, it doesn't mean you would have chosen the change, but you're acknowledging this is the way your world is. Coping implies you start developing new strategies and ways of dealing with your world and the changes you've experienced.

Not reaching acceptance and coping leaves you in a state of suspended denial, depression, grief, and guilt, unwilling to change how you live your life. Like Miss Havisham in Dickens' *Great Expectations*, the clocks will be stopped. Your life will be stopped. You'll be so stuck in your depression, grief, and guilt that you will not move on. Unwilling to accept what has happened and to change how you live, you'll be forever held hostage by his evil behavior. Acceptance and coping mean acknowledging the new truth of your life, seeing what it is rather than what it could be, should be, or you would like it be. And then acting on that new understanding.

Transformational Coping

Coping is the word used to describe the process of dealing with what has happened to you. You can react by steeling yourself, bracing your feet, and waiting for the next blow, or use what I call mental martial arts: transformational coping. In my tae kwon do classes our master teaches us to deflect an assault, and use the power of the attacker back against him, instead of just standing there and letting the blows rain down. Transformational coping lets you use the power of your crisis to increase your ability to deal with it. When a crisis occurs, you make the commitment to resolve the issues, take control where you can, and see the situation as a challenge rather than a threat.

COMMITMENT: Commitment addresses how you approach new situations, challenges, and risks. If you approach a difficult situation with curiosity and engagement, rather than by avoidance or by ignoring what is happening, you will be more effective in dealing with the challenge. Commitment is both a perspective on life and a decision. Some people habitually avoid and deny, withdrawing from difficulties. They pretend everything is okay, or it will be okay if they just don't talk about it. They put off the hard parts, hoping they will go away. Others find they do better by getting in there and getting the job done. Instead of waiting until the last minute, hoping the difficulties will go away, they get them out of the way first.

CONTROL: In this context, control means doing what you can, rather than trying to do everything. In every situation, no matter how complex, no matter how constrained, there is something you can do, something you can take charge of, even if it is just your feelings or thoughts. Control means acknowledging you *can* make a difference, and then looking for those opportunities where you can take charge.

Taking control in this way means that you have to give up trying to be in control. You need to stop trying to fix things long enough to stand back and see what is going on. You need to stop seeing the situation from just your own self-serving perspective, and move to a disinterested, more objective, perspective.

Not being invested in a particular way lets you see the opportunities for action. It is truly a paradox. The less you try to control, the more control you actually have.

CHALLENGE: In some ways, challenge is the hardest shift to make. Seeing a situation as a challenge, rather than a threat or disaster, can be a struggle. But it is an essential struggle to master if you are going to take charge and not let this situation ruin your life.

I can remember one "friend" telling me that I would look back on this experience and appreciate the pain, for it would make me a better person. I wanted to hit her. Looking back, I can tell you honestly that the immediate experience of the pain has dimmed with time, but I certainly don't appreciate it. Was my life changed by this experience? Absolutely. I am not the same person I was. Am I stronger and more confident? Yes, but I sure wish I hadn't had to pay the price.

TELL YOURSELF THE TRUTH

Starting a recovery process means telling yourself the truth about what's going on, taking that fearless inventory of what your life's all about and acknowledging, good, bad, or indifferent, this is what it is. Telling yourself the truth means admitting what you've done, what needs to be done, who you're responsible for, and who you're not responsible for.

Truth, for those of us who have been enmeshed in situations that are shameful and difficult, is hard. Oftentimes it is more attractive or more compelling to fudge, to pretend, to hope for things to be different, rather than admit the way they are. Unfortunately, this is what keeps you stuck.

It is also tempting to tell others what they want to hear rather than how you really feel and think. You might be trying to placate your spouse and protect yourself. You might be trying to protect others from the intensity or the content of your own feelings and thoughts. Or, you might be trying to protect your children from what has happened. There are lots of reasons offered for not telling the truth. Regardless, it keeps you stuck, unable to get on with your own recovery.

Telling the truth is hard. And it can be unpleasant. Telling the truth means telling yourself the good, the bad, and the ugly. Telling the truth means admitting you are better than some people, worse than others. It means you will disagree with some people and you'll have to challenge yourself to figure out what you really believe and what you just go along with. Telling the truth means you'll realize that you don't believe everything your parents, teachers, and religious advisors taught you. Telling the truth means you will discover who you are, the person behind your family roles of wife, mother, daughter, daughter-in-law; and your social roles of student, patient, friend, employee, boss, volunteer.

Telling the truth doesn't necessarily mean telling everybody everything that you know, particularly when dealing with your spouse, and especially if you are involved in the negotiations and the logistical hoops of extricating yourself from the situation. It may be important to think strategically about what you are willing to disclose.

Telling yourself the truth also means making the choice to protect yourself. There are some people whom you can't trust. With those people, you need to choose carefully what to say and what not to say. Deciding for yourself empowers you with your truth. You choose what you know, feel, and believe to be the truth. You don't blindly accept what others say is true for you.

Telling the truth means acknowledging what is, not what you want to be, not what used to be, not what he said was going to be, but what is.

Use the following exercises to start telling yourself the truth.

What Do You Do?

Make a list of ten to twenty things you've done in the last week.

If money was not an object, which of these would you have not done? Still do?

If no one was watching, which would you have not done? Still do?

If you knew you would not be alive in six months, which would you have not done? Still do?

What's Your Opinion?

Choose an issue that has a variety of viewpoints:

- Abortion
- Health care
- Religion in schools
- Death penalty
- Homelessness
- Welfare reform

Make a few notes about your opinion of the issue, how you think and feel.

Ask yourself:

- How do you know what you feel and believe?
- How do you know what the "other side" feels and believes? Where did you get your information?
- Which side is the truth? How do you know for sure?

It is usually easier to examine how you know what you know and how you have developed your opinions by looking at an issue farther away, one that doesn't directly touch your everyday life. Knowing how you know and how you have developed your beliefs in the world is the first step in deciding if what you "know" is what you believe, or if it is what you have adopted full-measure because it is what you were taught. It starts the process of deciding what thoughts are yours and what are others.

Acting on Your Values
- Family
- Friends and community
- Education/learning
- Spirituality
- Health
- Work
- Leisure
- Finances

Use this list of life experiences to help you define your values.
Rank the list from most (give it a 1) to least important (give it an 8).
Make notes to yourself on how you act on these values.

For example, education is very valuable to me, in the top 3 or 4 of my life values. Education means learning and challenge and fun. I act on this value by reading, reading, reading. I like to think about new ideas, talk to others about what I am thinking and reading, and do logic problems. I always have six to fifteen books checked out of the library.

Deciding What's Good
Knowing what you want and need is an essential part of knowing who you are. Ask yourself:

- What do you need?
  for survival
  for satisfaction
  for abundance
- What do you want?
  for satisfaction
  for abundance

Knowing what is "good" is the basis of morality. Philosophers have struggled with this question for centuries. Their ideas have varied incredibly. Their answers form the foundation for choosing what action you take and how you judge yourself and others. Some say if you want it, it is good. Others say if it feels good do it. Still others say if you need it, it is good; if you want it, it's sort of good.

What you want sometimes isn't all that good for you, or good for you in the long run. There was a time I ate more than was good for me. I didn't get really fat. I just anesthetized myself with food. I would come home from work, sample while I was cooking dinner, eat again with my family for dinner, and then fall asleep in front of the television. I wasn't having fun, I was in a fog. I wasn't seeing friends or getting things done, especially resolving some very uncomfortable problems in my life. What I was doing, trying to escape my problems, wasn't good for me. Using overeating as a bandage for solving my problems wasn't good for me either.

Think back over the last week.
How has what you've done reflected your needs? Your wants?
Did what you do get you what you needed? What you wanted?
What does this tell you about what you might do next?

Questions to Ask Yourself
How are you still accepting responsibility for what he did?
How are you letting it be his responsibility?
How are you still trying to change him, waiting for him to change, waiting for this to blow over?
How are you still pretending you don't feel what you feel?
At what level and with what issues are you still stuck in passivity?

Telling yourself the truth is acknowledging what is—not what used to be, what should be, what you want, or what could be. Only by being really clear as to what is happening in your life, right now, can you start to make effective choices about what action you need to take.

Telling the truth means facing your feelings—good, bad, and indifferent. It means treating yourself and your feelings gently, not judging yourself for the feelings that well up inside you. It also means understanding the difference between the feelings you have and what you choose to do. We may not be able to control our feelings, but we have an obligation to control our behavior.

FACING THE TRUTH
_____

Telling ourselves the truth means acknowledging the difference between what we say and what we do. In lots of ways it is easier to talk about what we believe, what we value, the choices we make. Looking at the obvious differences between what we say and what we do allows us to test the truths in what we have been saying. If we're just "talking the talk" and not "walking the walk" then what needs to be changed is clear.

Chapter 7

Making
Choices

*One of the most significant findings in psychology in the
last twenty years is that individuals can choose the way
they think.*

— Martin Seligman, *Learned Optimism*

After reading about making choices, complete this exercise on making
choices. Start the exercise now. Make a list of ten things you "have to
do," obligations you have, actions you are responsible for, in the space
below. These may be things you have to do every day, once a week, or
once in a while. They need to be things you don't have a choice about,
things that must be done, and must be done by you.

Obligations List

1. _____

2. _____

3. _____

4. _____

5. _____

6. _____

7. _____

8. _____

9. _____

10. _____

If telling yourself the truth gives you a starting point in taking charge of a situation you can't control, making choices is the base on which you stand as you take charge of your life. There is no way you can control your spouse, your children, your friends, the courts or the media. People will continue to do what they do, sometimes with seeming disregard for the truth, your feelings, and/or the impact their actions will have on your life. Trying to control them means you are trying to make them do what you want, to consider you/and others in their decisions, and to tell the truth as *you* see it.

You can't control them, what they think and feel, or what they do. You can try to influence them, to manipulate them, to coerce them. But ultimately other persons will do what they decide to do.

However, you can take charge of how you think, feel, and act in any given situation. Taking charge means you actively make choices about events or actions you *can* change, the things you do have control over. Taking charge means dealing with issues about which you have a say. As you are starting to take charge of your life, little things may be a big enough challenge: cleaning the house, responding to your attorney's request for financial records. As the crisis abates, you may see larger tasks that need to be accomplished: shelters to be organized, new legislation that needs to be passed.

The biggest difficulty in making choices is knowing when a choice is possible. If we act as if we don't have a choice, we will feel out of control, not in charge, and disempowered. If we acknowledge choice is possible, we increase our feelings of having mastery over our lives. Throughout the period of dealing with a case of child molestation, the choices you will be called upon to make are staggering in their consequences.

THE PARADOX OF CHOICE

Most of us say we want to have choices in our lives. We like to think we are in control, that we can decide what to do, and that we choose those with whom we associate. And yet we often act as if we have no choice at all, even when we do have a choice. Our behavior and our statements are contradictory: we say we want choice, and then deny we have it.

When Althea found out her husband had molested her younger sister, she said she wanted to leave him. But her husband said he had prayed to God for forgiveness. God had forgiven him, he told her, so how could she not forgive him? How could she leave him, if she was really a good Christian like she professed to be? Didn't she take a vow to stay with him for better or worse? Althea's faith was very important to her. Given this perspective, she decided she had to stay with him; she had no choice. She wasn't free to leave.

Shawna's husband had a long history of molesting neighborhood children. She said she had to stay with him. She loved him. She had no choice. She knew he had done terrible things, and really didn't approve of what he had done. But, she loved him. What could she do? She couldn't help how she felt.

Susanne had no love left for the man she married. When she found out he had molested several neighbor children over a ten-year period, she wanted to leave him. She knew she could make it on her own and she was furious with him. She had been dissatisfied with their marriage for a long time. But if she left, she would be admitting that her mother was right. Her mother warned her at their wedding that he was a bum, and that their marriage wouldn't last. So she convinced herself she had to stay. She couldn't let her mother be right.

All three of these women saw themselves as having no choice. They had to do what they were doing. There was nothing else they could do. They were stuck. They were not free to do what they really wanted to do. It was necessary to do what they were doing. There were no alternatives.

Seeing Choices

Seeing that you have a choice is the first step in moving from necessity to freedom. In his book, *How People Change*, author Alan Wheelis talks about the difference between freedom and necessity, and the paradox of choice.

Freedom, he says, is acting from choice. It includes the events, actions, attitudes, decisions, and accommodations we choose to make. The forces determining these choices are internal. They are inside ourselves. Necessity occurs when those same items are determined by forces outside ourselves. We can't make a difference with events caused by external forces. We can only alter events when the determination is internal.

Everyone experiences both freedom and necessity.

We can and do make many choices every day. We act on our freedom. We experience internal control. We make trivial decisions: what time to get up in the morning; whether to put our jeans on left leg first or right leg first; what to eat for dinner; or what style clothes we wear. We also make significant decisions: what career to pursue; whom to marry; whether or not to have children; whether or not to stay married; and in which part of the country to live. All these decisions reflect our freedom. With freedom, we feel in charge, our self-esteem increases, and we feel more confident. We feel powerful and empowered.

We also act out of necessity. There are things we can't control. Many events, situations, and decisions are determined by forces or people outside of ourselves. And these events impact our lives. Again, some situations where we have no choice, where we act from necessity, are trivial: the drugstore is out of our favorite shampoo, so we buy another brand. Other situations of necessity can be life-altering: a drunk driver hits your car and you are severely injured; you are awarded, or rejected, for a fellowship for career training; or your husband molests children.

When acting from necessity, we usually feel out of control and not in charge. Our self-esteem decreases. We feel less confident about our ability to get things done. With necessity, it is easy to feel victimized. Someone, or something else, is determining how our lives will be lived. We feel powerless and disempowered.

Wheelis goes further and describes two types of necessity: arbitrary necessity and objective necessity. The differences are subtle but very important. They provide the key to how to feel in charge of situations you can't control.

OBJECTIVE NECESSITY: Objective necessity occurs when you *really* can't control what is happening. Objective necessity includes situations that are caused by natural laws: genetic determination; who your parents are; gravity; the color of the sky; earthquakes.

These determinants are not personal. Gravity does not exist just to make your life difficult. It doesn't exist to annoy you when you slip and fall and hurt your elbow. When you personalize objective necessity, you increase your feelings of victimization. With personalization, you believe you are the cause or the targeted victim of an event. The earthquake happened to you. A root exists so you can walk down a path and slip on it. From personalizing the event, it is a short step to taking responsibility and blaming yourself for making it happen.

I grew up in California where earthquakes are common. I experienced several moderate to severe earthquakes as I was growing up. When I moved to Chicago, there was an earthquake there, even though the city seldom experiences earthquakes. When I moved to Massachusetts, there was an unusual earthquake. Sure enough, when I moved to metropolitan Washington, D.C., there was another unusual earthquake. I teased my friends to follow me; I make the earth move. Do I really cause earthquakes? Of course not.

The consequences of previous situations or actions are also included in objective necessity. For example, I cut my shin badly in a fall when I was a child, and again when I walked into a glass door as an adult. Both cuts left scars on my leg. I can't go back to that previous time and erase either of these cuts. I may have plastic surgery to minimize the scars, but I can't now make the cuts not have happened. They did happen. The scars are current consequences of those cuts.

I can be annoyed at myself for tripping over a root and falling when I was a child. I can be angry that the local hospital did not suture the cut because I was not eligible for care, and so it took much longer to heal and left a much larger scar. I can promise myself to be more careful while walking in the woods, or when checking to see that a glass door is open before I try to walk through the doorway. There are things I can do now to minimize the consequences of the accidents and how I feel about the scars, but I can't go back now and make my leg not be cut. It did happen. I have no control now over whether or not it happened.

A cut leg is trivial. Being married to a child molester is not. The consequences are not trivial either. And, just like the cut, you can't go back and make it not happen. There are scars, remnants, and reminders of the event. There are also undeniable consequences of being married to a molester. The event has an undeniable impact on your life.

So too with your spouse's molesting. You can't go back now and make it not have happened. As much as you want it not to have happened, it did happen. And, there will be consequences; you will have scars. No matter how angry, sympathetic, depressed, or sorry you feel, you can't go back and change the past. And, like the cuts on my legs, there are things you can do now to minimize the consequences of being married to a child molester by changing the way you think and feel about the situation and yourself. It has a lot to do with how you deal with arbitrary necessity.

ARBITRARY NECESSITY: Arbitrary necessity includes those events, situations, choices, decisions, and attitudes that we believe are controlled by outside forces, but which are really under our control. These are the situations in which we *act as if we have no choice, but we really do.* Arbitrary necessity is even harder to deal with than objective necessity.

We invent arbitrary necessity. We make it up from our understanding of the lessons we have been taught in life, the values of our church, the values parents and teachers held up to us, and our own fears, feelings, and dreams.

Arbitrary necessity is rooted in shoulds: you should call your mother every day, you should put others' needs and wishes ahead of your own, you should be a good wife.

Arbitrary necessity is nourished by values: this is how to honor your mother, how to be a good friend, how to be a good wife. Arbitrary necessity is based on the rules and decisions we use to mold and guide our everyday behavior. And we all need rules and guides. The important thing to remember is that they are just guides, guides that we have chosen.

What makes arbitrary necessity tough to deal with is the whole issue of responsibility. When we deny our freedom to make choices, we also deny our responsibility for acting as we do. We can't help it, we tell ourselves. We have no choice, we explain to our families and friends. We have to. We deny our freedom to choose so we can act like we think we should, or how others think we should. We deny our freedom to choose so we can do what is socially acceptable, or religiously correct, or nice. We deny our freedom to choose because we think other people know better than we do what is best for us, or are entitled to being in charge of us. We buy into someone else's definition of what is right or true about our lives.

Althea denied her freedom to make a choice about staying in her marriage. She let her husband define what she should do as a good Christian woman. Even though she could have made a case for his being un-Christian, for his behavior being immoral and unacceptable, she let him define what she should do, how she should feel, and how she should live her life. Then she acted on his definition. She was stuck in arbitrary necessity. She thought she had no choice. She acted as if she had no choice. But she really did have a choice. She chose to stay.

Shawna denied her freedom when she attributed her actions to being in love. *Love made me do it* is the theme of country songs, not the theme of a woman in charge of her life. From her definition of love, a woman stood by her man no matter what. Shawna was a "prisoner of love." She was stuck in arbitrary necessity. She didn't realize there are many other definitions of love. She thought hers was the only one. She thought she had no choice. She acted as if she had no choice. But she really did have a choice. She chose to stay.

Susanne was caught in a particularly difficult trap. Separating from our parents is a shift that we all have to make as we become adults. When we are kids, our parents exert control and direction over our lives. We either agree and adapt to their wishes, or we disagree and rebel against them. In either case, our parents control our behavior. If we do what they want us to do, we put them in control. If we do just the opposite and rebel, we are still choosing our actions in response to their wishes.

Susanne thought that if she did what her mother wanted, her mother was in control. She was struggling with the difference between the process and content of decision-making. Freedom depends on the process of choosing freely, not on the content of the choice. If Susanne could evaluate the situation, see her husband's behavior as unacceptable to her, and choose not to share her life with someone she finds reprehensible, then she would be able to exercise her freedom.

If Susanne evaluates the situation, sees her husband's behavior as unacceptable to her, and makes the choice to stay with him so that her mother won't have the satisfaction of being correct, then she has succumbed to arbitrary necessity. She has the freedom to choose, but she feels like she can't choose. She is denying her freedom. She is stuck in arbitrary necessity. She thinks she has no choice. She acts as if she has no choice. But she really does have a choice. She chooses to stay.

CHOICES YOU MAKE

Go back and look at your list of things you have to do from the exercise at the beginning of the chapter. If you are similar to most people who do this exercise, you will have both objective and arbitrary necessity items on your list. Some things you really have to do, others you really choose to do. Circle the items that you really *have* to do.

Did you circle things like breathe, sleep, and eliminate? Or did you circle things like pay taxes and bills, mow the lawn, put on make-up, or change the kitty litter pan?

I know what you are thinking: "I have to pay the bills and taxes. I have to mow the lawn. I have no choice."

The point of this exercise is to recognize you have much more choice than you acknowledge. We all tell ourselves we have to do what we do, denying our freedom to act on choice. Other than the involuntary life functions, such as breathing, sleeping, dying, and eliminating, we choose everything else that we do.

Kitty Litter Principle

Usually most people acknowledge that most of the items on their list are choices, not necessities. Even if the task is unpleasant, they choose to do it because the consequences for not doing it are worse.

But one day, Beth, a woman I was counseling, insisted that changing the kitty litter was a necessity, not a choice. She had to change the kitty litter every day. I was fascinated. Never before had I met someone so committed to kitty litter. So I asked her what was the worst thing that could happen if she didn't change the kitty litter. Beth explained that she had a new relationship in her life. She also had an old cat whom she dearly loved.

As you might guess, the new man in her life didn't like cats. More specifically, he didn't like kitty litter pans. She feared her new love would get so upset about the kitty litter smell that he would leave. If he did leave, she would never have another relationship and would end up dying alone and lonely.

At this point Beth started to laugh. She realized just how silly her reasoning had been. It was highly unlikely that her relationship would be broken by a smelly litter box, and yet that was how she was acting.

Confronting Arbitrary Necessity

The questions that I used that day to confront Beth's lack of choice with kitty litter are summarized below. When you find yourself acting as if you have no choice, use this pattern of questioning to determine how you have denied your freedom and are keeping yourself stuck in the perception of lack of choice.

When you find yourself saying, "I have to . . ."

Ask yourself:
What would be the worst thing that could happen if I didn't do what I think I have to do?

Challenge your answer:
How likely is it that what I fear will actually happen?

In the kitty litter case, the likelihood of Beth being alone for the rest of her life was very low. She had been worrying about something that was probably never going to happen.

Then ask yourself:
Why is what I fear, even if it is likely to happen, so bad?

If you're truly honest with yourself you'll see that nothing is ever 100 percent bad, or good. In the worst situations there are some benefits; in the best situations there is usually something negative. In the kitty litter case, Beth realized if her man did leave she'd have no more fights over kitty litter! In other words, the benefit to her for not changing the kitty litter was a more peaceful living arrangement.

Kitty Litter Principle Questions

What's the worst thing?	*How likely is it?*	*Why is it so bad?*
Dirty kitty litter.	Very slight.	He'll get annoyed.
He's annoyed.	20%	We'll have a big fight.
We have a big fight.	10%	He'll leave me.
He leaves me.	10%	I'll never have another relationship.
I'll never have another relationship.	15%	I'll get old and die alone.

This process of questioning the results of your decisions can be very powerful to uncover the irrational thinking that keeps you stuck in negative situations or relationships.

Theresa was stunned when she discovered that her husband of many years, a junior high school teacher, had molested three of his students. Her worst fear was that she would be blamed for his behavior. As we worked through her fears, she realized that it was very likely that she would be blamed for what he had done. In answer to why that would be so bad, she could only say that it would be awful. She kept saying she wasn't responsible for what he did, and wanted everyone else to hold her blameless. She didn't want to be shamed by his behavior. Finally she realized when she was blamed that she would know who her true friends were. They would be the ones who didn't blame her.

Theresa was blamed by a good many people for her husband's molesting. Some "friends" even said if she weren't so aggressive and extroverted he wouldn't have had to turn to his students for attention and "love." Looking back on the experience three years later, Theresa now realizes the act of other people blaming her for his behavior was a turning point for her. Knowing she didn't deserve the blame, and that she didn't need to accept this judgment from "friends," she could stop accepting the responsibility for his behavior.

Theresa now sees that what upset her so was what psychologists call projection. She was blaming herself for his actions, and was attributing the blame to other people's comments. When she heard them say she was responsible, she was able to let go of her unreasonable acceptance of responsibility. She now realizes that having terrifying fear come to realization was incredibly liberating for her.

Knowing you have acted from choice, not necessity, makes hard tasks easier. As you go through your recovery process, there will be many opportunities to grapple with tough choices. If you are driven by necessity, feelings of resentment and anger are inevitable. If you acknowledge you have choices, you can take charge of situations you can't control.

One of the most difficult issues I dealt with was the custody of my son. I very much believed it was in the best interest of my son for me to have full, permanent custody. There was considerable evidence his father had molested several of his friends, was still doing it, and denying he was doing anything wrong. The newspaper headlines were promising to explode with all the graphic details.

Meanwhile, the base of my business had shifted to the opposite coast. Most of my work was out of town. Yet, I felt strongly that teens need stability. I also felt very strongly that my primary task was recovery, both his and mine. He was just finishing junior high. I had four years to help him heal before he left home to face the world.

The complexity of the decision was staggering. But, as I focused on what was important to me, what I felt I needed and what my son needed, the answer became clear.

His recovery was prime. He needed and deserved a resident parent who could provide for him. He did not deserve to be battered by newspaper headlines about his father.

So, I worked for full custody, and as soon as it was final, moved the two of us to a community near my major client, stopped traveling for business, and focused my energy on parenting a wounded teenager and a wounded woman. There were times he drove me nuts, times I didn't want to be the only parent, times money was tight. But, I knew I had made a good choice, and the right choice.

It is not easy to embrace freedom of choice. It is understandable why some people want to back away and retreat into arbitrary necessity, rather than face the responsibility of choice. But, there is a price for denying your freedom. When you act as if you have no choice, deny your choice, and deny your freedom often enough, soon you will not have it. Your freedom will be gone, and you will not know where or how or when you lost it.

IN CHARGE, IN CONTROL

The one thing we can always take charge of, even in situations in which we have little, if any, control, is our *reaction* to what happens. While it is easy to experience your feelings as being out of your control, or as connected to the event rather than to you, you can take charge of your feelings too. It is not so easy to realize that not everyone feels the same way you do about what happens in life.

In a support group one evening, Carol was furious with Louise. Louise had been explaining why it was impossible for her to hold her husband responsible for having molested several children in the youth group he sponsored at their church. She knew his mother had been sexually abusive to him as a child and that his father would get drunk and beat him badly. Louise focused on how Stan had been treated by his parents and felt it was their fault he molested the children. He couldn't be blamed. He was a victim himself.

Carol confronted Louise, saying there was no excuse for Stan's behavior. He was the adult, he had responsibilities to the children, their parents, and their church, and there was no excuse for what he did. She didn't care how badly people had been abused as children, as adults they are now responsible for their actions.

Both Louise and Carol were convinced their reactions to the situation were the right ones, and everyone would agree with them. As we discussed and processed feelings that night in the group, it became clear to all the participants that no *one* feeling was connected to the event, and that each of us brings his or her own experiences, values, and interpretations to the issue.

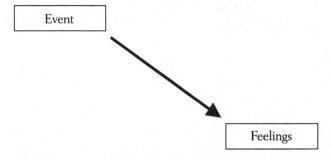

Louise and Carol were acting as if their feelings were directly connected to what happened, when in fact there is an interpretation step. For the most part, interpretations are very quick, automatic, and out of our awareness. And, because they happen so quickly, it is easy to miss them, or to not realize how they belong to us, rather than to the event itself.

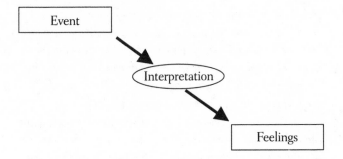

Louise had a very different interpretation of Stan's molesting than Carol. For Louise, Stan's early experiences mitigated his responsibility for his behavior. Because his parents had abused him, she was not holding him responsible in the same way Carol was. For Carol, Stan was totally responsible, no matter what his prior experiences had been. This event aroused very different feelings in the two women and his behavior had two very different meanings. They had both fallen into the trap of assuming everyone would have the same reaction to the event as they did. It is not true.

PROBLEM-SOLVING AND CHOICE

It is very typical to have a preferred problem-solving style—a favorite way to react and then take action when challenged by a difficult situation. Some people withdraw, go to their rooms to think about it. Others jump in the car and run home to their mothers. Others look around for an expert to solve it.

Jackie Schiff, a therapist known for working with the most challenging of mentally ill patients, outlines a model of passivity that explains how people approach problem-solving. Her model is particularly applicable to situations in which there is a feeling that someone else caused this situation and it feeds into a feeling that there is not much you can do to change it.

Schiff's model for passivity takes on four stages:

- **Stage One, "No Problem":** At this stage, there is no conscious awareness that any kind of a problem exists. Oftentimes, other people can see a problem, they may even mention it to you, but you just don't see anything as being wrong. This is the no problem position.

- **Stage Two, "Nothing Can Be Done":** The problem is acknowledged. Yes, it's a problem, it is a serious problem, but there's nothing that can be done that's going to make a difference. The problem is essentially unsolvable. Not just unsolvable by you, but by anyone. This is the no solution position.

- **Stage Three, "Maybe Someone Else":** At this stage, there is an acknowledgment of a problem existing and that it has a solution. But not a solution you can do. You believe at this stage that you are not smart enough, not capable enough, or not strong enough to be able to solve the problem. Other people may be able to do it, but not you. This is the disempowered position.

- **Stage Four, "I Can Take Care of This":** At this stage, there is an acknowledgment of the problem, recognition of the seriousness of the problem, an awareness that it does have a solution, and a feeling that you can solve it. This is the empowered position.

Using Schiff's model, you can assess how and where you are keeping yourself stuck by not solving the problems you have. Are you still denying there is a problem? My ex-husband denied to the day he died that he had ever done what he had been accused of. The problem wasn't his actions but rather other people picking on him, not believing in him, and legally harassing him for no good reason.

Are you denying a solution to the problem? Sometimes I feel this way about how society can get molesters to stop doing what they do. I just don't see how the solutions we've tried have been successful, whether it is a twelve-step program, or long-term insight psychotherapy, or incarceration. None of the treatments work. I'm pessimistic anything will ever work. I'm stuck at a no-solution level with this issue.

Getting stuck at the third level of passivity is very typical for spouses of child molesters. They can see others who have had the same experiences, and how others have made significant progress in recovery. They just can't seem to do it for themselves. They see the problem. They see a solution. But, they can't see themselves using the solution. They stay stuck.

Then there are those who empower themselves and get on with their lives. They don't discount the seriousness of the problems, nor their pain and anger. They see the solution and they go after it. They take charge and don't let their husbands' behavior ruin their lives.

The hardest part of problem-solving is trying to figure out what problem you are trying to solve, and then thinking through all the different ways of looking at that problem. Use the following pointer questions to make sure you have thought about all the different aspects of the problem:

- What is the problem?
- What results do you want?
- What do you believe?
- What do you know?
- What is your dream?

What Is the Problem?

How you define a problem determines the solutions you will find and/or apply. The reasons you give for an event will determine the actions you take as a result of that event. If you define your partner's problem as turning to children for sexual release because you weren't sexually available to him, you may choose to be more sexual with him in an attempt to get him to turn his attention to you, not the children. If you define his problem as a consequence of the abuse he experienced as a child, then you may get angry at his abusers, be sympathetic to his victimization, and encourage him to go to therapy, or even go yourself. How you define the problem leads to your next steps, whether the definition is accurate or appropriate or not.

What Results Do You Want?

When defining a problem, ask yourself what results you want. The results you are looking for will point you to the appropriate action to take. If you are working on a short-term, one-time project, you might want to do a "quick and dirty": quickly take action to finish the project. How you do the work might not matter as much as just getting it done. If you are working on a long-term project, with expectations of doing more, or similar, work in the future, you might want to spend more time setting up the process for doing the work than actually doing the work itself. Even though you are spending more time on the planning and setup, it pays off in the long run. If the results you want are to have your partner out of your life, the actions you take will be very different from those you will take if you want to restore your relationship with him. If you aren't clear about the results you want, or can't decide which of two conflicting results you want, you will keep yourself stuck.

What Do You Believe?

This question addresses issues of the assumptions, inferences, and premises you use to frame the problem, and the way you look at the problem and possible solutions.

- Assumptions are the factors of the problem that you think are true . . . or the factors that you take for granted. Most of us don't even think about the fact that we are making an assumption, and that is how the assumptions get us into trouble.
- Inferences are the conclusions you draw from what you know and believe. It takes your knowledge to the next step, from what you know to be true to what you think must happen next. Sometimes you are right, sometimes you are wrong.
- Premises are the rules you use as guidelines for structuring your thinking, what you assume (there's that word) to be the way things should be. Again, most of us usually don't question the premises we use, and again, we can get ourselves into trouble.

Let's go back to Louise and Carol. There was no disagreement on what Stan did, just on how to interpret his actions. Louise saw Stan as a victim. From this perspective, she inferred that her next step was to be sympathetic and supportive of him as he dealt with the legal and social consequences of his behavior.

Louise's Perspective

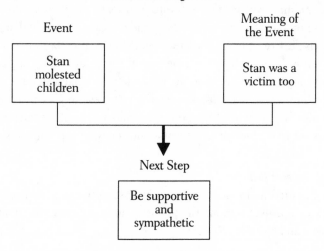

Carol didn't deny that Stan had been abused as a child, but she didn't accept that abuse as a reason for his not being responsible for what he did to the children. From Carol's perspective, her next step was to hold Stan responsible for what he did and expect him to pay the legal and social consequences for his behavior.

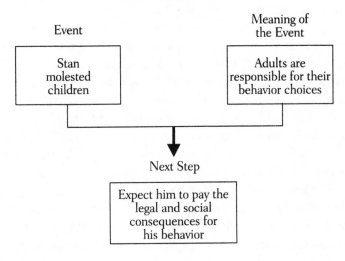

Carol's Perspective

Event	Meaning of the Event
Stan molested children	Adults are responsible for their behavior choices

Next Step

Expect him to pay the legal and social consequences for his behavior

What Do You Know?

Collecting data lets you gather the information you need to solve your problems and organize your work. Here is where lazy thinking can really get you in trouble. If you aren't careful, you will see what you want to see rather than what is really there. The rule is look, and then look again. You may even need to take a break and come back to see more clearly what is, rather than what you know should be there.

You don't need to do a scientific study with control groups and random samples, but it is important to collect information from a variety of sources. Even "facts" are colored by the opinions and biases of the people who offer them. People with good intentions and your best interests at heart may not be sufficient sources for you. What has been true for others may not fit you, or your situation. This is especially true when dealing with social services, and the legalities of your situation. Protect yourself by investigating fully. Think it through.

Thinking it through means being logical about the problem. Apply systematic, logical rules to thinking ahead about what could be true. Logic can be helpful when you don't have all the information you need. But be careful. Logic can trip you up. Just because it is logical, doesn't make it true, or even possible.

When you start to read books and articles about incest and/or child molesting be especially aware of the backgrounds and theories the authors hold. The beliefs of a particular author will be evident in the reasons he or she gives for why people do what they do and how you, as a family member, are involved.

Two books that offer a good contrast are Patrick Carnes' *Out of the Shadow* and Stanton Peele's *The Truth about Addiction and Recovery*. Both are probably in your local library. Take both books off the shelf, find a quiet corner in the library, and skim through them.

Carnes designed and developed an inpatient treatment program using a family systems model of treatment. He sees sexual acting out as an addiction and twelve-step programs as the only/best treatment modality. His program treats the wife as well as the husband, considering her as much responsible for the sexual dysfunction in the family as him.

Peele, on the other hand, does not hold an addiction view and is not impressed with the efficacy of twelve-step programs. The treatment program he designed is based on his belief that the disease model of addictions is not only incorrect but hinders or delays recovery. Instead, he proposes a model of treatment that builds on people's own strengths, values, and confidence in themselves and on their relationships with family and friends, while teaching them skills which will improve how they deal with their lives. He proposes that the way you need to deal with "love addictions" or recover from trauma is by believing in yourself and your ability to act in your own best interests, while actively, slowly but surely, changing your daily habits and behavior patterns to support more effective life choices.

After carefully reviewing the two books, you can see that even the experts in the field have different opinions and operate within different parameters. The challenge: Don't accept without investigation the first model you find and try to fit that model. Keep looking until you find the model that fits you.

What Is Your Dream?

Dreaming taps into the flow of your creative thoughts. Creativity is the creation of the new, or the rearranging of the old in new ways. It challenges you to consider what could be, not just what is. Even though your creative ideas may be outrageous, they may have a kernel of possibility that you can use. The problem with most people is too little creativity, rather than too much. Brainstorm solutions with your friends, or members of your support group. The objective is to come up with as many new ideas as possible in the time allotted, without censoring any suggestions, however bizarre. Later, you can evaluate ideas for reasonableness, practicality, and relevance.

For example, other people in Carol and Louise's group had lots of creative suggestions as to how to handle the situation. Listening to the variety of suggestions, they all realized that there is seldom one solution to a problem. Although some of the suggestions were quickly discarded, such as public humiliation, Louise realized that her husband did have to publicly acknowledge what he had done even though it may mean revealing his own abuse.

DECISION-MAKING

Be careful not to get yourself into analysis paralysis when you are working through problem-solving. It is seductive to keep gathering data, keep thinking issues through, hoping that you will get to the position where the way will be self-evident. While that may sometimes happen, don't count on it. More often than not you will have to make a decision. You will have to choose what to do next, even though you don't have all the information you would like, and when the way is not self-evident. Making a decision is what you do when you don't have all the information you may need, and certainly want.

To make a good decision you will need:

- A number of different alternatives
- Consequences to each alternative
- Criteria that permit the consequences to be ranked

When these conditions exist, you can make a decision. You need to have a number of alternatives, certainly more than two. If you stop at two, there is every likelihood that you will miss an alternative. You also need to know the consequences of each alternative, as best you can. You can't predict the future with certainty, but a best guess based on data is important. You also need to have some criteria. The criteria are based on what you know and what you want. It goes back to the desired results question. I had already been considering divorce when my husband was first arrested. Then, I felt stuck. I had to either go completely or stay wholeheartedly. It took awhile to realize that I had the option to go ahead with the separation and give him moral support as he was dealing with his crisis. This third alternative was the one I chose. At the time, as I considered the consequences of each alternative, I was sure that if I got a divorce others would interpret my divorcing him as a signal that he was guilty. But, I also knew one of the consequences of staying was getting further enmeshed in a marriage that was already over. I thought by leaving and supporting him I would achieve the results I wanted: a divorce that would not tear both of us and our son apart. It was my best decision based on what I knew, believed, and wanted at that time. But, I couldn't accurately predict the future.

This process seems rational, and yet the difficulties that many people have in making a decision involve dealing with the emotions and feelings that may be attached to the problem, the alternatives, and/or the consequences.

To become effective at the decision-making process, it is necessary to differentiate between decisions and outcomes. The decision is the act of selecting from among alternatives. The outcome is the result of the act of choosing. While you have control over the decision, you don't have control over the outcome. Making good decisions will increase the possibility of good outcomes, but there is no guarantee.

Questions to Ask Yourself
- What do you tell yourself you have no choice about?
- Do you really not have a choice?
- What hard choices have you had to make?

- How are you still seeing yourself as responsible for what he did?
- How has that made a difference in what you choose to do?
- How do you see him as responsible for what he did?
- How has that made a difference in what you choose to do?
- Look again at the problem-solving passivity model. You will be at various stages depending on the issue.
- What issues do you have at each level?
- Are there some things that you don't see as a problem, yet other people tell you they are?
- What are the things you take care of automatically?

Making choices means acknowledging that you do have a choice, that you can decide how you want your life to be, the guidelines and values you will use, and how you live out your values. Sometimes, we choose to do things we would prefer not to do—like pay taxes or obey the speed limit—because the consequences of not following the rules are so unpleasant. But, for the most part, the choices we make reflect our wants and wishes. By acknowledging we are acting from choice, we feel more empowered, feel more in charge of our lives, and experience more life satisfaction.

Fear, especially fear of unlikely, worst-case consequences, can keep us from acting from our choices, or from addressing and resolving the problems we have or the decisions we need to make. By challenging ourselves to take each step in the problem-solving, decision-making processes, we are able to move forward and take action that will implement the choices we make.

Chapter 8

Making Changes

Courage is the capacity to go ahead in spite of the fear, or in spite of the pain.
— M. SCOTT PECK, *Further Along the Road Less Traveled*

Empowerment is a popular concept both at work and at home. Numerous articles and books have been written on how managers and supervisors might empower their employees to be more responsible, to take charge, and to feel more connected to the work they're doing. When we look at empowerment within the context of our personal lives, there is no manager or supervisor to facilitate the process. We find ourselves placed in the position of being both the manager and the participant.

> *Katie struggled with feelings of low self-esteem, low self-worth, and low self-confidence. She knew that she wanted and needed to make some changes in her life and was searching for someone to tell her what to do and how to do it. She confided in her friend Richard that what she needed was to be empowered.*

She explained to him the only problem was there was
no one around to empower her. Richard listened attentively
to his friend's anguish and then quietly commented that
what might be more appropriate than looking for someone to
empower her was for her to consider herself empowered.

As Richard said to Katie, we need to consider ourselves empowered and to start acting as if we are. Empowerment means living your life on purpose. You know you are in charge of your life. You choose how you react to situations. You decide what your life will be. You are the expert on you. It doesn't mean you can control everything, but rather you can take charge of how you think and feel in situations you can't control.

For spouses of child molesters, empowerment is a problematic and difficult task to accomplish. To consider yourself empowered means that you can tell the truth about your life, you can acknowledge what has happened, and you can be aware of the impact your experience has had on you. Many spouses of child molesters have had to acknowledge and accept the concept that the men they married have deep psychological and emotional issues, and that at some level they were held in thrall by their spouses. Telling the truth means dealing with the shame, the guilt, the grief, and the deep hurt of having been so betrayed.

Many women recognize they have wittingly or unwittingly given up their self to someone or something else. To be empowered means that you no longer live your life for someone else, and you no longer let other people define who and what you should be. You acknowledge that you can make your own decisions about your life, and that you do not need to depend upon others for your definition of self.

It is helpful for your recovery to recognize the cues that tell you when you're feeling disempowered. Many people experience discomfort in the diaphragm, sweaty palms, and a rapid heartbeat. Others want to sleep a lot and find themselves avoiding social contact. Many say they experience an internal argument that goes around and around in their heads, robbing them of sleep and resolving nothing. If you can recognize the symptoms of being in conflict with yourself—that there is a discrepancy between your behavior and your goals, that you are not living assertively—you need to work through the turmoil and gain use of your power again. You don't have to ask for permission or wait for somebody else to empower you. You start to understand and recognize that you have both a responsibility and a right to reclaim the individual you truly are.

Struggling with the concept of disempowerment inevitably leads to discussions of what situations or people have crushed your spirit, shadowed your power, and encouraged you to be less than who and what you could have been. Everyone has her own story of difficulties, hard times, and often tales of abuse and mistreatment by parents, spouses, siblings, or friends. Of course, each one of us can point to a distressing, demeaning, and/or destructive situation that we experienced. However, some people are crushed by their experiences, and others, whose experiences have been just as difficult, find them empowering. What is the difference? How can one person rise above a difficulty yet another is crushed by similar or even less noxious events?

It was this question that propelled Marty Seligman from his research on learned helplessness to focus on what he calls learned optimism.

LEARNED OPTIMISM

After uncovering learned helplessness in his animal studies, Seligman went on to study how this phenomenon occurred with people. In these studies with people who had experienced traumas and/or experienced abusive situations, about two-thirds of the participants learned to be helpless. And, one-third of them didn't. The question was, what made the difference in the response to trauma in these two groups of people?

What Marty Seligman and his colleagues at the University of Pennsylvania found was little if any difference between the experiences that their subjects had. It wasn't what happened to them that made a difference, but how they interpreted what happened. He called this their explanatory style, or the meaning they attached to experiences they had. He divided his participants into two groups—those people who *were not* crushed by their experiences, whom he called learned optimists, and those people who *were* crushed by their experiences, whom he called learned pessimists. He found three factors in the explanatory style of learned optimists that differentiated them from the explanatory style of learned pessimists. The three factors were how permanent they thought their situation was, how pervasive they saw the situation, and how personally responsible they felt for the occurrence of the situation.

Permanence

Permanence is the temporal factor, the timing of the situation. The situation can be temporary or permanent. From a temporary perspective, a person might say to herself, Yes, I know it's difficult today, I'm really uncomfortable, I don't like what's going on, but this too will pass; soon things will get better. If an individual has a permanent perspective she might say to herself, Yesterday was bad, today is awful, and tomorrow is going to get even worse; there is no end to all the difficulties I am having, this is going to go on forever. As you might start to guess, learned optimists see their difficulties as *temporary* while learned pessimists have a tendency to see their difficulties as more *permanent*. No matter how bad the situation is, the optimist is convinced things are going to get better. The pessimist, on the other hand, is convinced that no matter how bad the situation is today, tomorrow's going to be even worse.

Pervasiveness

Pervasiveness is the measure of how specific or how universal a particular situation is. It addresses how widespread the impact of a difficulty will be on a person's life. Some people are fairly specific in seeing the effects of their difficult situations. Just because one thing is going bad in their lives doesn't mean that everything is going bad. They can put boundaries around their situations or encapsulate their difficulties and not let them spread over to other areas. They see the impact of their problems as specifically affecting only one area of their lives.

Other people see the impact as much more universal. If they are having difficulties at work, they believe things will go bad at home. If they're having difficulties with their spouse, they'll also expect to have problems with their parents, friends, children, or co-workers. For these people, problems in one area of their lives quickly invade all other areas of their lives. If one thing goes wrong, everything goes wrong. Learned optimists more likely see their problems as specific. They can keep them contained rather than let them spread out to all areas of their lives. Learned pessimists are much more inclined to see their problems as universal.

Personalization

Personalization addresses the source or the cause of the difficulties a person might be experiencing. The focus is either external, "Something outside of me caused this problem," or internal, "I did this. I made this awful thing happen." Optimists and pessimists have different understandings of the external or internal causes of both positive and negative events. In general, optimists are more inclined to see positive events as being internally caused, and attribute negative events to happenstance or bad luck. On the other hand, pessimists are more likely to attribute positive situations to happenstance or good luck and negative things to something that they caused themselves. Either perspective allows for people to fool themselves and not to acknowledge their responsibility for the events of their lives.

It is understandable that in the midst of reacting to finding out that your spouse has been molesting children, you would take a pessimistic view of your life and situation. But recovering from the crisis, being able to put your life back together, means you will need to take a more optimistic perspective. Your situation is not permanent. No matter how it feels at the moment, things *will* get better. You will stop feeling the pain so acutely. There will come the day when you will be able to make the decision that I did, that your life will not be ruined by what your partner did.

Being the spouse of a child molester will not fill up your life forever. You will see experiences and places that are not influenced by him. You will develop new friends, start new activities, not feel so ashamed that you hide who you are, or not feel so raw that you tell everyone you meet what has happened to you. Not because you are ashamed, but because it is old news.

And, most importantly, you will develop a perspective on what is yours and what is not. You will start to identify those things that you can control, those things you can influence, and those things that truly are luck and/or happenstance.

To consider yourself empowered involves changing the ways in which you see yourself, as well as relearning to handle the challenges of everyday life. Your empowerment is reflected in your optimistic or pessimistic approach to life. At a base level, the attitude of empowerment is one of an actor, or being proactive in your life, in contrast to being a puppet or a reactor to situations, forces, and people around you. You see yourself as being able to make things happen, not waiting for things to happen to you. You can see the good and the challenging at the same time. You can balance positive and negative experiences against each other. And you know that nothing lasts forever. Change is an inevitable part of life, and you know you have the flexibility and skills to deal with both the changes that come your way and the changes you choose to make. Making this transition from puppet to actor, from reactive to proactive, is essential as you consider yourself empowered.

Empowerment is closely aligned with both self-esteem and assertiveness. You see yourself as both worthy and capable. These skills are self-reinforcing: they are characteristics of empowerment and generate further empowerment. The more effective you become at assertiveness, the more empowered you will start to feel. The more empowered you feel, the more effective you will become at assertiveness.

EMPOWERMENT AND SELF-ESTEEM

Self-esteem, how we feel about ourselves, affects every part of our lives. The experiences and opportunities we have, and our reactions to them, are shaped by the level of our self-esteem.

Without positive self-esteem, we miss opportunities, or don't take full advantage of the opportunities that are available. Life is difficult and painful. With positive self-esteem, we confidently reach out to new challenges. Relationships flow more smoothly. Life satisfaction and joy increase.

When you have been through the trauma of being married to a child molester, your self-esteem has often been battered. Many women report they feel less of a woman, are no longer confident of their own competence, are sure they aren't as smart or attractive as they thought they were. How they feel about themselves has decreased dramatically. But, no matter what level of self-esteem you are experiencing, it is possible to grow in self-esteem. Is possible to increase your own self-esteem.

Sound Self-Esteem: What It Isn't

Self-esteem is a balance between expectations and perceptions. Expectations include what you think you should do, or should be, as well as what others think you should be. Perceptions are the judgments, the evaluations of how well you are living up to your expectations. When expectations are in balance with perceptions, positive self-esteem results.

Expectations are shaped early on by parents, teachers, other children, religious instructions, and social/cultural forces like the media. Later, spouses, friends, and relatives add their expectations. Most people pick and choose the types and levels of expectations they have for themselves from these early experiences. Typically, expectations women have for themselves are high. So high, that they may be impossible to meet. For most women, perceptions are much lower. Most women judge themselves harshly, as they are constantly not meeting the expectations they set for themselves.

A strong self-esteem is based on loving yourself just the way you are. This doesn't mean you don't want to make some changes or grow. It does mean you aren't waiting to feel good about yourself until you're perfect. Loving yourself means self-acceptance, recognizing both your strengths and your limitations. Many spouses of child molesters struggle to understand the difference between loving themselves and being selfish or narcissistic.

SELFISHNESS: Ironically, being selfish is not loving yourself too much, but too little. The selfish person is so sure everyone else has more than she does, she sees herself as lacking the basics, and she is sure she hasn't gotten what she deserves. So, she tries to make up for what she doesn't have by taking from others—or keeping what little she does have to herself. Selfish people think so little of themselves they try to take from others to build themselves up. But, it doesn't work. Taking from others just highlights how little they really have. And, no matter what they take from others, it is never enough or the right thing to fill the empty gap inside.

NARCISSISM: Narcissism is pathological self-involvement. It is self-love taken to destructive limits. Narcissists are shortsighted, focusing on what feels good at the moment, what is expedient, not what will be good in the long run. The criteria for decision-making is either "If it feels good do it" or "No one is going to tell me what I can do." With this approach, consequences are often not considered. What counts is today, not tomorrow. With relationship shortsightedness, there is no depth of commitment or connection. People, possessions, and jobs are seen as disposable and replaceable. The rules here are "It doesn't matter" and "There is always another if this doesn't work out."

Narcissists seem unable to see themselves realistically. They are always the greatest. They are always confident, sure their view of any situation is accurate. They exaggerate their strengths and minimize or deny their limitations and/or the negative consequences of their actions. They are unable to get feedback from others, or hear that there may be another way to do the task at hand because they just know their way is the right way.

EXCESSIVE HUMILITY: Even more destructive to self-esteem and more common with spouses of child molesters is excessive humility. Everyone needs some humility, it is what keeps a person honest and human. Appropriate humility acknowledges limitations and flat sides. It allows you to assess your strengths and talents realistically, understanding that there are usually people more talented or more skilled, as well as those less talented or less skilled. This assessment is taken without shame or blame, but as an assessment of what is.

But, taken to the extreme, excessive humility is negative narcissism. No one is worse, more wrong, less skilled, more shameful than you. Your assessment of self is inappropriately harsh. Excessive humility can also lead to assuming the blame for all the ills of the world, or thinking the world is ganging up on you. You see yourself as either totally persecuted and/or as responsible for anything bad that happens to anyone. Or, you see yourself as totally victimized, responsible for nothing. It all happens to you. Either position denies your responsibility for being in charge of your life, and the responsibility others have for their lives. The choices you make, the actions you take, are yours. With the belief no one is worse than you, you stop yourself from being who you can be.

Characteristics of High Self-Esteem

Characteristics of high self-esteem are self-reinforcing. The behaviors that reflect high self-esteem promote more self-esteem. The more you have, the more you develop. People with high self-esteem:

- Are confident. They know they are competent, and take action based on their confidence in their competence. They use their expertise in one area on challenges in new areas.

- Respect themselves. They know who they are, they accept themselves, and don't make excuses. People with positive self-esteem respect others. They realize they can feel good about themselves without needing to be in a "one-up" position. They do not need to put other people down to feel good about themselves. For people with high self-esteem, there is plenty of room at the top.

- Trust themselves to make and keep commitments, set goals, and follow through. They keep their word and expect others to do so also.

- Are resilient. High self-esteem allows you to meet challenges and flexibly deal with them. Instead of being buffeted and defeated by adversity, you can meet the challenges and not be defeated.

Increasing Your Self-Esteem

The question then is: Is it possible to change your self-esteem? If it is possible to increase self-esteem, who does it? Do you need someone else to do it for you? How do you keep yourself on course while you're changing? Where do you start? How do you do it?

You can start to increase your self-esteem today. You don't need to wait until someone else changes their behavior or apologizes for treating you badly in the past. You don't need them to be different for you to change yourself.

The simple answer to the question, Can you change your own self-esteem?, is that you are the only one who *can* do it. No one else can do it for you. Others can be supportive, give you feedback, and make suggestions of what to do. But changing your self-esteem is a do-it-yourself project. You don't have to do it *by* yourself, but you must do it *for* yourself.

Some people may react to the changes you make, both positively and negatively. Those close to you will enjoy and celebrate the changes. Others may be threatened, angry, or frustrated by the changes you make.

> *Aileen knew she weighed too much. She needed to get more exercise and cut down on the amount of fat in her diet. She knew she no longer had the beautiful body she once did. But, she also knew she had been working hard during the time of crisis after her husband's arrest. She had finished a job-training program and found a job with benefits after being a homemaker for over twenty years. She gave herself three months on the job to settle into a routine and then she would tackle her weight. One thing at a time, she said.*

To maintain a sense of self and change yourself at the same time is a challenge. Like trying to stand on a moving floor, you must pay attention to subtle, constant changes, you must constantly shift and adjust so you can keep your balance. The balance you maintain will be dynamic, not static. What was in balance yesterday may not be balance tomorrow.

MAKING CHANGES

Forming the base for the balancing act is a secure knowledge of self, values, beliefs, and how they are expressed. Essential, too, is the understanding that, although actions and behaviors may shift, the values they express remain stable. Life changes bring change of behavior.

Knowing where to start the process of changing and increasing your self-esteem can be difficult. Don't let indecision, while finding the best place to start, be the stumbling block that stops you from taking action. When it comes to increasing your self-esteem, the concept of multicausality is in operation. Any one of a number of different roads can lead to your destination. In some ways it doesn't matter what you do first. Start where you are—start with the easiest thing to change—start where you have leverage.

Starting with the easiest means choosing those projects that have the greatest likelihood of success. When it comes to increasing self-esteem, nothing succeeds like success. Even a small, discrete step, carried to completion, helps start the energy flowing. Taking charge and making change happen is another one of those behaviors that is an indicator and enhancer of self-esteem.

Leverage includes any factors and influences that can give you a positive edge. Is there a project that is close to being finished? Do you have a skill or talent that will make the achievement of a goal more likely? Is there a support person who can assist? Start there.

Purposeful Self-Talk

How can you improve your own self-esteem? Sound self-esteem involves maintaining a balance between the expectations you have for yourself and the perceptions you have of yourself. For most people, the expectations they have are unreasonably high, and the perceptions they have of themselves are unrealistically low. To improve self-esteem, you can either decrease your expectations, or improve your perceptions. To speed up your progress, you can do both.

To decrease expectations or improve perceptions, you need to change both what you think and feel about yourself and how you express those thoughts and feelings. You need to change your "self-talk."

Everyone uses self-talk all the time. It is the automatic, inner voice that comments on our behavior, feelings, and thoughts. For the most part, the comments are critical and, especially if we are feeling down or discouraged, distorted. Automatic self-talk typically mirrors the earlier messages we have heard, regardless of how inaccurate or outmoded they may now be, and often play over and over again in our minds like bad tapes.

To improve perceptions, to decrease expectations, you will need to insert the interpretation/analysis step described on page 126 to pick and choose which messages to accept, and which ones to reject. The content issues also need interpretation and analysis. What information is accurate, inaccurate, current, relevant, useful? To improve unrealistically low perceptions, to decrease unreasonably high expectations, go beyond simply thinking positively and disregarding negatives. By using purposeful self-talk and adopting a more optimistic perspective, you can improve your self-esteem.

Purposeful self-talk adds the interpretation/analysis step. Instead of stopping with the automatic response, you challenge yourself to recognize the logical flaws and self-sabotage, and replace them with more rational and appropriate responses.

Self-Talk Exercise

Automatic self-talk is what you say to yourself about an external event, your own behavior, or what you are thinking or feeling. Use purposeful self-talk to interpret and analyze automatic responses.

Format is important in purposeful self-talk. Start with a personal pronoun; then your name; and then a specific, positive, active statement of what you do or who you are. For example:

I, Cindy, am careful and conscientious.

Be sure to use positives. When you say, "I am not sloppy," it reminds you that you are—or have been—sloppy. Keep it positive—where you want to be.

Confronting Automatic Self-Talk

Choose an automatic self-talk message that you often say to yourself, for example:

"I'm just not good at detail work."
Revise the statement to make it purposeful, positive self-talk.
"I, Cindy, am careful with the details of my work."
Now write the response that you make to this new statement:
"Sure, that's why you can't balance your checkbook."
Then reply to the negative remark. Argue with yourself.
"My checkbook is in the best shape it's been in for years."
Continue with responses and replies, defusing the automatic negatives with purposeful positives. Use the following format to guide your own argument:

Automatic self-talk statement:
Purposeful self-talk:
Response:
Reply:
Response:
Reply:
Response:
Reply:
Response:
Reply:

Soon you will find that the responses you make lose their charge and become less angry and disparaging. The new, purposeful self-talk phrases you use start to feel comfortable and accurate. As you get more skilled with confronting automatic self-talk, a shortcut can be to simply say, "That's not like me anymore" when you catch yourself repeating an automatic self-talk message. Used consistently, challenging automatic self-talk is an effective tool to help you start to change the way you see yourself.

Positive Self-Esteem Habits
While confronting negative self-talk and taking a more optimistic perspective are the primary methods of increasing self-esteem, habitual behaviors can also help confront unrealistically low perceptions or unreasonably high expectations. When you are feeling low or depressed, it is more common to get stuck in negative thinking. Even though you may not feel like it, even though you don't want to, practic-

ing the following self-esteem habits can help pick you up out of a destructive and disempowering cycle.

- **Focus on your strengths today.** Acknowledge what you do right, your talents and skills. Look at how far you have come, rather than how far you have to go.

- **Give yourself credit.** You have made a difference, your choices and actions have shaped the results you've accomplished. It wasn't just luck. It was *you.*

- **Treat yourself as your own best friend.** You wouldn't say terrible things to your friend, shame her in public, curse her, or call her stupid. Stop being hurtful to yourself, and treat yourself with the love and respect you extend to your best friend.

- **Put your best foot forward.** Pay attention to how you dress, your hair, your house, your desk at work, and the work you do. Present yourself as good as you'd like to feel about yourself. You may even want to buy yourself some flowers, or spend your lunch hour getting a manicure.

Self-esteem habits also are useful in decreasing unreasonable expectations. Develop the following self-esteem-enhancing habits:

- **Make mistakes.** Perfectionism is one of the most destructive factors for positive self-esteem. Expecting perfection means you will seldom, if ever, measure up. You will always fail. (This does not mean be mediocre. Just be human. Acknowledge you aren't, and can't possibly be, perfect.)

- **Say no.** You don't always have to put others first. You don't always have to accommodate others at your own expense. It is okay to decide to say no.

- **Say yes.** Treat yourself, give yourself rewards for "good behavior." (But be sure those treats are true rewards. Spending money you don't have on items you don't use is sabotage, not rewarding yourself.)

COUNTERING SELF-ESTEEM ASSAULTS FROM YOUR SPOUSE

Dealing with a negative, demeaning, or emotionally unbalanced spouse is a particular challenge to maintaining sound self-esteem. If your spouse has been defining you and your life, if you have been in thrall to him, letting him take charge of who you have been, it will be especially difficult to rebuild your self-esteem. He may have used anger and rage to frighten you into accepting his views of what you should be, or built on your own natural feelings of shame and guilt to tear down the good feelings you had about yourself. Or he might have taken a righteous position, taking the higher moral ground, and judging you as a sinner or "less-than in the eyes of God."

Relationship Rules

The relationship beliefs you subscribe to will shape how you confront your spouse's assaults on your self-esteem. Two beliefs, in particular, are especially toxic: the belief that he is special, and you're not; and the fear that without him, you are nothing.

The belief that he is special and you are not is a cornerstone belief for people with negative self-esteem. It has far-reaching consequences. Putting him in the "one-up" position automatically puts you in the "one-down" position. It is like being on a teeter totter. He can only be up if you're down. He knows more than you, is a better judge of what is right or true, and can make better decisions that you. It's a short step from these beliefs to allowing him to make decisions for you and about you. You see him as being in a better position than you are to guide the course of your life. He, not you, is in charge of your life.

The fear that without him, you are nothing, is a direct consequence of believing your spouse is better than you, or better able to run your life. In turn, the consequence of this fear is the belief that if you aren't good, he will leave. Of course, the definition of good is what is pleasing to him. The fear is that if you hurt him or disappoint him or aren't who he wants you to be, he will leave; then you will be nothing. This leads to placating behavior, not speaking up during disagreements, or letting the other person take advantage of you.

Countering both of these relationship rules or beliefs challenges you to use all the self-esteem-enhancing suggestions in this chapter. Your objective is to get off the teeter totter and develop a relationship where the value and worth of both people can be acknowledged.

Use positive self-talk to affirm your strengths, to refer to yourself in more positive, less derogatory language. Take time to practice self-esteem habits, to give yourself credit, and to treat yourself as your own best friend. Acknowledge that you can think through issues and challenges, that you do know how to run your own life, and that while you may *want* to help your spouse as an important part of your life, you don't *need* him to survive.

BREAKING OUT OF UNPRODUCTIVE BEHAVIOR

One of the most effective tools I use in counseling sessions is the "Drama Triangle" created by Steven Karpman. The Drama Triangle is a Transactional Analysis tool that describes behavior patterns that are repetitive, nonproductive, and often lead to conflict or uproar among the participants. Karpman's model describes how people react to one another, especially how they try to make others responsible for their own feelings and actions. It is a model of disempowerment in which a participant takes on one of three roles: victim, rescuer, or persecutor.

Victims

Victims hang out looking for either somebody to kick them or someone to help them. They can be spotted by their whining tone of voice, helpless look, hanging heads, and shuffling feet. They look as if they don't know what they are supposed to be doing, and often describe themselves as being "overwhelmed." Victims aren't happy unless they are miserable. Victims are caught in the second or third stages of passivity. They are painfully aware of their problems but either don't see any solutions or a solution they can implement. If they are really stuck, they will resist the efforts of others to help them, preferring to stay in their favorite miserable feelings rather than get on with their lives by solving their problems.

Victims also tend to have an external focus of control, and see everything they do as arbitrary necessity. Their problems are caused by other people, the weather, the media. The list is endless. All their problems are external. They also have no choice. They have to do what they're doing. There is no way they can change their responses to their situations.

Drama Triangle

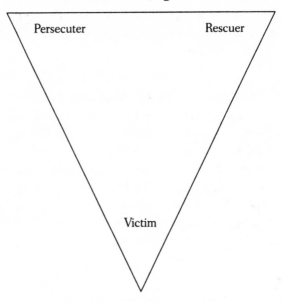

Persecuter   Rescuer

Victim

Rescuers

Rescuers inflict help on people. They aren't happy unless they are helping someone else, typically at their own expense. Unfortunately, their help usually isn't the right kind, isn't appreciated, and their advice isn't followed. When they get to feeling bad, it's for not being good enough.

Many spouses of child molesters, like many other women, find the rescuer role comfortable and familiar. They are the family caretakers. They run after victims, helping before they are asked, putting others in their debt in the process.

Marilyn knew she was a rescuer. The family teased her about finding every bird with a broken wing. Her kids said she inflicted her advice on them. In the support group, she started to realize how she would help others even if they didn't want help. Then she would stand back and observe with a sigh, it was always up to her. She hadn't realized how she was keeping others in her debt by helping everyone, and then setting herself up as a martyr by refusing offers of help herself.

Persecutors

Persecutors aren't happy unless they're blaming others. They are usually seen as unreasonable, demanding, and ruthless. They blame their victims for asking for abuse, and then deny responsibility for their own hurtful behavior. If others would just be different, they could change too. But in the meantime, there's nothing they can do.

The Drama Triangle is a dynamic model. People move from role to role with incredible rapidity. The drama is played out in predictable practiced patterns. A participant usually starts in a favorite role, but then moves to other roles as the situation demands and the game plays out.

An interaction between two people may start with the victim hanging her head and looking for help and the rescuer rushing in to help. When the help doesn't work or isn't good enough, the rescuer starts feeling like a victim, helpless and hopeless. "Nothing I do is ever okay," he says to himself. The victim sees this as an invitation to move into the persecutor's position and reply, "Yep, I knew you couldn't help me. You people are all alike."

This round is over, with the rescuer determined to help better and the victim more certain there is no solution to the misery.

For years, I used Karpman's model to describe dysfunctional interactions, helping people understand how they got caught up in unproductive, disempowering interactions with family and friends. As I started to focus more on how people empower themselves by taking risks and making choices, I realized there are many powerful, effective behaviors hidden underneath the dysfunctional surface. If people could access these more positive actions by recognizing their choices and the meaning that they attributed to the events that shaped their behavior, they would experience more empowerment.

Counselors

Each role in the Drama Triangle has its counterpart in the Empowerment Triangle. The empowered role of the rescuer is counselor. Counselors are supporting and nurturing. They are interested in win-win relationships, where people take care of themselves and collaborate on taking care of each other. One of the most important pieces of shifting from rescuer to counselor is the counselor insisting upon doing less than 49 percent of the work when asked for help. Doing less than 49 percent of the work means the other person retains responsibility for the results. It is still the other person's job and not yours. When you do more than half of the work, you are almost always in rescuer mode rather than counselor mode. You've made the success of the outcome dependent upon how skilled and competent you are. You've also let the other person off the hook.

The other very important process in shifting from the rescuer mode to counselor is unhooking yourself from being personally invested in the outcome. This is the "hard love" approach that many parents find necessary in dealing with their acting-out or substance-abusing teenagers. It is a survival skill that the best therapists and counselors develop. From this perspective, you assess your contribution, independent of what the other person does or does not do. You acknowledge and recognize that you cannot control and change someone else, that you can only do what you do.

Many times I have watched clients in counseling sessions struggle with making changes or confronting their abusers, only to choose to stay in the same relationship and pattern of behavior. I couldn't assess my competency as a therapist on the content of their choice, only on the process of their choosing wisely. My responsibility was to provide an environment for healthy change, one that would encourage an appropriate, expected, or freely chosen decision, but not for a particular choice to be made. I could not be responsible for any given choice, since everyone has his or her own free will, and is responsible for the decisions he or she makes. If I kept the process clear and provided encouragement and support, I was doing a good job.

Empowerment Triangle

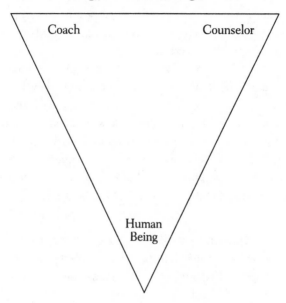

Coach

Persecutors make the shift to empowered behavior when they choose to become a coach. Coaches give honest feedback, set limits, and define boundaries. Coaches push back and challenge us to take a careful look at our expectations, ask for clarity, and set criteria for results. Coaches are pragmatic in defining boundaries. Coaches are critical, not in the sense of being negative, but in the sense of being careful. They look at the facts and reality, not at a fantasy world of what should be.

Human Beings

As the group was developing the Empowerment Triangle, we were stuck with what to call the person who moves from victim to a more empowered position. My colleague, Catherine Seo, made the comment, "We should probably call them 'human beings', because isn't that what we all are?" Anyone can find herself in a situation where things are not going the way she wants them to or there is so much going on she can't cope with it by herself. The difference between the victim and the human being is that the human being asks for what she wants and takes responsibility for herself. In that position, as a human being, you recognize and create options and choices for yourself rather than expecting someone else to create them for you.

You don't have to do it all by yourself, though. Human beings typically take one of two positions, and where they look for help depends upon the type of help they want. If they are looking for sympathy or are dealing with the feelings of the situation, they'll look to the nurturing counselor for support. If they are looking for solutions and actions, the coach is the person they need. The question "Are you looking for solutions or sympathy?" will often trigger the shift from victim and allow a person to get on with being a human being.

SHIFTING FROM DRAMA TO EMPOWERMENT

Making the shift from unhealthy behavior within the Drama Triangle to positive, healthy behavior within the Empowerment Triangle occurs by acting on choices. You can choose to:

- Deal with reality, deal with what is rather than what you want, look at the here and now, or, as Jack Webb used to say in "Dragnet," look at "just the facts ma'am, just the facts."

- Trust. Trust in yourself and trust in other people. Trust yourself to function as an adult, be optimistic about the nature of humankind, understand that people have choices, and that sometimes people choose to do nothing.

- Take a collaborative approach, recognizing we are all in this together. Collaboration means being responsive to the others rather than responsible for them.

- Shift the context from who's right to *what's* right, to what will solve the problem, rather than assigning blame.

- Take the risk, or as the saying goes, "Feel the fear and to do it anyway." The only way out is through, you just have to do it.

Moving out of drama and into empowerment is transforming. You will feel more energy, more satisfaction, and more joy in your life. You will be able to think more effectively and clearly access both your intuition and logic. You will be open for growth and opportunities, able to take advantage of the opportunities that are available.

Breaking out of unproductive behavior is at the heart of empowerment. It means choosing your behavior, rather than being on automatic pilot. It means looking at what you have been doing, acknowledging that you need to make changes, and increasing your skills so you can be more effective at simply being a human being.

ASSERTIVENESS SKILLS

Assertive communication skills are the first skills to develop. They help strengthen both your self-esteem and your interactions with others. Acting assertive before you start to feel assertive helps you develop the skills to an automatic reaction. Give yourself some time to practice and become proficient.

To behave assertively is to validate your personal power. It is exciting when you know what you want and can express it. You feel balanced and your energy level is high. Your body is not stressed by conflicts between your feelings and your thoughts. You know that you are on target.

How often do you find yourself doing something you do not want to do—sitting watching a movie you do not want to see, eating Chinese food when you really want Mexican, cleaning closets when you want to go hiking, going along with another person's definition of your life? By not asserting your wants and giving away your power, you quietly step into watching the movie, eating the Chinese food, cleaning the closet, and going along to get along. And you feel disempowered.

For example, when an assertive person is invited to go out for Chinese food, she responds, "I would enjoy seeing you and meeting for dinner, but I don't want Chinese food tonight. If you really want

Chinese food and would like to ask someone else to go out with you, I'll understand and take a rain check."

If the person who extended the invitation is also assertive, she may respond, "I really do have my heart set on having Chinese food tonight so let's make plans to get together soon. I do want to spend some time with you."

In the above examples, the point is that being assertive doesn't mean every person or group of people will go along with what you want. Just as you have the right to assert your wants, so do they. If, in order to meet your objectives, you need people to agree with you and to say yes to your every request, you are likely to be very disappointed, feel out of control, and be upset much of the time.

You may know people who use their power to force others to comply with their wishes. This is aggressive behavior. Author Patricia Evans in her book *The Verbally Abusive Relationship* calls it a "power over" position. On the other end of the scale are those who give away their power and go along with the wishes of others. This is passive-compliant behavior. People who give their power to others spend a lot of time feeling frustrated or disappointed. They want others to be able somehow to anticipate their needs and know what they want, without their having to speak the words. They may dream of ideal relationships with no conflict and lots of accurate mind reading. As they give in and go along with others, they wait for the same consideration. As they wait, frustration turns to anger and resentment, often directed at themselves.

Empowerment is about reclaiming personal power. The choice is yours as to how to use the power you have. You can give it away. You can bully other people with it, or you can be true to yourself—recognizing, validating, and stating your wants while allowing others the right to do the same. You can empower yourself by being assertive.

Self-Esteem and Assertiveness

Self-esteem is basic to assertiveness. They feed off one other. An assertive person speaks and acts with assurance; she is in touch with her power. An assertive person is able to communicate her wants and needs.

As you give yourself permission to articulate your wants, you increase dramatically your chances of getting your needs met. Stating your wants and effecting a change validates you to yourself. As a result you satisfy your needs and increase your self-esteem. Paradoxically, even if your needs aren't met, you will still feel better about yourself for having asserted yourself. You have better than a 50 percent chance of getting what you want when you state your needs. If you fail to assert yourself, your chances drop to about one in ten.

Shortly after I separated from my husband, he took our son on a weekend outing. We had agreed they would be back by 5:00 P.M. on Saturday. Five o'clock came and went, and they weren't back. I knew where they had gone, and I knew there were plenty of phones along the way home, but no one called and no one came. Finally, they showed up at 9:30.

I was furious. I told my husband that being late and not calling was unacceptable. My plans were ruined and he was being inconsiderate. He tried to defend himself by saying it had gotten late and they stopped at a favorite restaurant for dinner. He knew they would be late, but what were they to do? Miss dinner? All I kept repeating was, next time he was to be back on time or call me and tell me. He kept asking if I wanted them to miss dinner. He never got it that it had nothing to do with dinner. It had everything to do with his expecting to be able to make or change arrangements that were convenient for him, and not consult or even inform me.

Even though my husband stalked off in a huff, angry, accusing me of not caring about whether they ate, I felt really good for standing my ground. He didn't need to agree with me, or even agree with what I asked, for me to feel good about myself.

Your own behavior and its consequences provide you with information about yourself, how you feel, and how others see you and feel. How you present yourself, whether you are assertive, passive, passive-aggressive, or aggressive, what you expect, and how you go about getting it are all connected to your level of self-esteem.

Appearances can be deceptive, however. You can appear to others to be assertive in situations where, in fact, you feel unsure of yourself. Conversely, you may appear unassertive when you feel that you are being assertive. Everyone has some experience in being assertive. You are reading this book. You are doing the work of your job. You are struggling with putting your life back together. With practice, you can learn to be assertive in those areas where you still have trouble. When you do so, your self-esteem will be enhanced and you will feel more empowered.

Assertiveness training helps you to identify and be aware of your strengths, skills, and accomplishments and share them with others. You have a choice in each interaction. You have a choice with each statement you make to yourself. Assertiveness training encourages you to take charge, to put yourself in control.

Assertive Communication Skills

Assertiveness is most often expressed verbally: what we say when we talk with others. Some of the message is nonverbal: how we hold our bodies and how comfortable or anxious we appear. Some of the message is vocal: the tone, pitch, and rate of our voices. When we can combine our verbal, nonverbal, and vocal messages congruently, saying yes, saying no, or just making an observation about the way we see the world, we assertively take our place as women entitled to have their own opinions and to take charge of their lives.

"I" MESSAGES VERSUS "YOU" MESSAGES: In being an assertive person, the focus is on self-awareness. If you take responsibility for your own feelings and behavior, identifying and stating clearly what you want, you increase your odds of achieving your objectives and goals. You cannot be assertive if you do not know what you want.

Starting sentences with "I" helps keep you on target. I statements clearly relate your position without imposing that position on another. With I statements, you validate your feelings and wants in a manner that does not confuse, accuse, or manipulate others. A statement starting with "You" often puts the other person on the defensive. When a person feels defensive, he or she is likely to tune you out, think of things to say to excuse him- or herself, or switch to the offensive and attack the speaker.

SAYING "NO": Some people have so much trouble saying no it is as if their mouths are physically unable to form the words. We easily fall into the habit of always saying yes to others, even when we don't want to. When we do this, we are letting others be in charge of our lives. And we feel disempowered. Remember, empowerment is based on the belief that you know yourself best and are in charge of your own life. You decide what's right for you.

- **Be as brief as possible.** Give a short, legitimate reason for your refusal, such as, "I really don't have the time." Avoid long, elaborate explanations, justifications, and lies, such as, "I can't because I think I have an appointment with a new therapist at that time, the kids need new shoes, and I have not finished my report for work yet . . . ."

- **Actually say the word no when declining.** The word no has more power and is less ambiguous than, "Well, I just don't think so . . .," Given an opportunity, many people will seize any hint of ambiguity and interpret your answer as not really meaning no. Say the word. Let them hear it.

- **Repetition and persistence may be necessary.** You may have to decline several times before the person "hears" you. It's not necessary to come up with a new explanation each time; you can use your original reason over and over again.

- **Shake your head when saying no.** Often, women unknowingly nod their heads and smile when they are attempting to decline or refuse, giving a double message. Make sure your nonverbal gestures mirror your verbal messages.

- **Avoid the words "I'm sorry."** Try to be conscious about using this phrase to excuse your refusal or otherwise weaken your credibility. (Habitual use of this phrase can be distracting to your real intent.)

SAYING YES: Saying yes often involves saying yes to yourself and saying no to someone else. Make sure you are the one who addresses the reasonableness of a request. Make sure it is reasonable for *you*, not just the person who is doing the asking. It is easy to slip into the belief that if someone asks you, it is reasonable. After all your best friend is a reasonable woman, she wouldn't ask you to do something unreasonable. Sure she would, especially if she knew you would say yes so as not to risk harming your friendship. You decide. Say yes to yourself, and don't give an automatic yes to everyone else.

- **Don't feel the need to offer an explanation when you say yes to yourself.** Just wanting it or just feeling like it is plenty of reason to treat yourself.

- **Think about what you want, not what you have always done.** My sister told me one of the fun things about her empty nest was not having to cook a big dinner for her family every night. Her idea of a good Friday night dinner is strawberries, Camembert cheese, wheat crackers, and a good bottle of wine. She usually tops it off with a chocolate cake. No veggies . . . just yummy finger foods that feed her soul as well as her body.

- **Don't get stuck thinking about what other people will say or do.** It is your life, you have spent enough time taking care of others. It's time to mother mama.

ASKING FOR A FAVOR: Asking for a favor from someone else is another form of saying yes to yourself that many of us have trouble with. Especially if we define ourselves as a favor-giver rather than the favor-asker. But, asking others to help us is a gift for them as well as for ourselves. It becomes a way for our friends and family to make their love for us visible.

Don't hedge and beat around the bush when you ask for help. Be direct. Let the other person know what you want, what you need, and what will resolve the problem for you. The other person can't help if he or she doesn't know what to do. Don't make the other person guess, give him or her all the necessary information. If you need help with baby-sitting Thursday evening, don't ask if the person has plans. Ask if he or she will baby-sit.

Don't feel you have to bribe someone to do something for you. It may well be that you can return the favor in the future, but keeping a ledger book on favors between friends is an excellent way to ruin a friendship. It evens out over the long run, not in the short run. And not necessarily in kind.

Give the person time to think it over. This means not waiting until you are desperate before you ask. Try to anticipate your needs, and then if the other person can't do it, you still have time to ask someone else or make other arrangements.

Don't apologize for asking. Everyone needs help sometime. This is your time. You are being reasonable aren't you? You aren't asking for something the other can't give, or for more than what the other can do, are you? Evaluate what your request will sound like to your friend.

Questions to Ask Yourself

- In what way are you stuck in a Drama Triangle relationship?
- What steps do you need to take to come from a more empowered position in this relationship?
- How good are you at boasting about how good you are? Can you:
  Describe your natural abilities?
  Claim your skills and accomplishments?
  Describe your best product or accomplishment from this last year?
  Tell what you are proudest of?
- Most of us are assertive, nonassertive, or aggressive depending on the situation and the people involved. Can you:
  Tell someone good things about you or your accomplishments?
  Ask for clarification of something you do not know or understand?
  Admit that you are wrong?
  Express your opinions or feelings when they are different from others being expressed?
  Interact with authority figures or people important to you?
  Ask for help or advice?

Respond to an unfair remark or criticism?

Tell a person he or she is doing something that bothers or
offends you?

Tell a person who has called that you are too busy to talk?

Empowerment is not magically bestowed on you by another, nor
is it just an attitude or feeling. Empowerment starts with recognizing
both where you are and where you want to be. Getting to where you
want to be means seeing yourself in a new way, letting go of outmoded
ideas you have about yourself and what you should be. You start to
build a new view of yourself by changing what you say about yourself,
what you say to others and how you treat yourself. You start acting as
confident, competent and successful as you would like to be. And, as
you change what you do, your feelings change too.

Chapter 9

Forgiveness

When we forgive, we transcend the pain we feel by surrendering our right to get even with the person who hurt us.

— LEWIS SMEDES, theologian

When you're in the midst of the hurt and hate that you experience as the spouse of a child molester forgiveness is one of the most difficult concepts to consider. The very idea that you'll someday be able to forgive your spouse for the pain and disruption that he's caused to your life is hard to believe.

The problem when defining forgiveness is everyone has a different idea of what it is and how to go about granting it. It's hard to sort out your feelings and come to some kind of acceptance and understanding of what you want to do for yourself around this issue.

Forgiveness is not something you do for *someone else*, but something you do for *yourself*. In many ways it's not even something you do for your own children or the children your spouse has victimized . . . they will have to forgive for themselves. Forgiveness is a way of taking care of yourself and freeing yourself so that you can get on with the rest of your life.

Forgiveness is a very personal process. Much of the work you will do will be done inside the thinking of your own head and invisible to the people around you. While you may use tools and techniques suggested by others—prayers and meditations, rituals, and therapeutic techniques—in the end, the forgiveness process you use will be uniquely yours.

What looks like resolution to one person may look like a half-way step to someone else. It is essential that you sort through the suggestions and techniques, the philosophies and theories, the admonitions and exhortations, around the idea of forgiveness and craft for yourself a forgiveness model that will be both effective and healing.

Be sure to consider not just how to forgive, but who you need to forgive and for what. Most of us find that we not only need to forgive our spouses but also forgive ourselves. We may need to let go and forgive other people—family members, lawyers, court personnel, and social service professionals.

Forgiveness takes time. We need to give ourselves the time we need to forgive, acknowledging and recognizing that forgiveness comes slowly, with difficulty and a good deal of effort and attention. Forgiveness is not something that you can do in one seminar, one reading of this book, or one afternoon of sitting by the side of the seashore, staring at the waves, letting your feelings flow out of you.

Forgiveness is sneaky too. Just when you think you finished, here comes the hurt and anger welling up inside you again. As I wrote this book, many of the old feelings came back. It is as if I need to take one more look to make sure it was all over.

FORGIVING FOR YOURSELF

Its absolutely essential to understand that the reason you forgive your spouse who has hurt you so badly is not for him but for you. You need to forgive him for what he did to you, how your life was impacted, how you were hurt, not for how he hurt other people, or more importantly, for who and what he is.

Heidi had tears in her own eyes and there were tears in many of the other women's eyes as Heidi told the story of her hurt and betrayal in a support group one evening. For many reasons, most having nothing to do with her, she was unjustly fired from her job as a college professor. She recounted the long list of hurts and conflicts that had preceded her termination.

It was very clear that the pain she was feeling was unjustly visited upon her, that she had become the victim of a nasty department chair and his need for power and control. Her termination had little, if anything, to do with her skill as a teacher or her expertise as a researcher.

Because the rules and format of the group precluded any questioning or conversation about the speaker's experience, I waited until the break to approach her to tell her how moved I was by her story and how aware I was of the pain she was experiencing. I also asked if she had been able to find a job teaching this year, what was she doing now. She looked at me with incredulity and exclaimed, "Oh, didn't you realize? The story I just told you happened ten years ago."

In no way do I want to diminish the pain and the anguish that Heidi was experiencing from her unjust termination. However, her experience, her reaction to it, and my understanding of what was going on with her scared the daylights out of me. It became for me a very important lesson on what happens to people when they hold onto previous wrongs.

Heidi's pain and anguish and her inability to focus on new activities were as fresh and clear in her mind ten years after the event as they had been ten days after the event. She had still been unable to get another teaching job, she felt her department chair had ruined her life, and that she was forever going to be hurt and unhappy. She was still holding on to the resentment and anger she felt toward him, still wanting the situation to change so that she could have what she wanted, her old job back.

Forgiveness Frees the Forgiver

Heidi's anger frightened me. I was so scared that I would hang onto what happened, that I would still be, ten years after the event, labeled as somebody who was "just the spouse of a child molester." I was afraid this experience would somehow expand to fill up my whole life, that I would never be free of it. I was afraid that even though the legalities of the divorce were finished, I would still be haunted by this experience.

Letting go of the experience, putting it into some kind of understandable framework, lets you get out of this stuck position. It lets you take charge of the situation that you haven't been able to control and not let it control you. Unless you take charge, you're unable to get on with the rest of your life. Until you forgive and let go you no longer have a life. Your life is that of being a victim.

Getting Stuck in Righteous Anger

Beware of getting stuck in righteous anger. Take a look at what you are holding on to, and why you are holding on. At one point I realized I was more committed to everyone knowing what a rat my husband had been than getting on with my own life. I kept trying to convince friends and acquaintances that he was the bad guy. I wanted other people to tell me I was right and he was wrong.

> *Jennifer kept waiting for her husband to admit what he did was wrong. She couldn't forgive him until he agreed that molesting their fourteen-year-old baby-sitter was wrong. He kept saying it was no big deal. The girl came on to him, she probably wasn't even a virgin, and so he wasn't the first. He had all kinds of good reasons it wasn't his fault.*

Jennifer got caught up in righteous anger. She knew she was right and her husband was wrong. He should own up to what he did, it was his fault, and he was wrong. So they quarreled and quarreled. She assumed it was her job to change him, to fix him. She was right, he was wrong, she had to get him to admit it.

Waiting for someone else to change, especially waiting to admit he was wrong, is futile. He won't and your life will be a mess while you try. You will be dead right forever, and make yourself miserable to boot. At some basic level, it doesn't matter who is right. What matters is you are letting his misbehavior ruin your life. Is that what you choose to do?

White Knights Don't Make House Calls

This is one of my sister's favorite sayings. She uses it when I am moaning and groaning about life not being fair, not wanting to take care of myself, and wanting a knight in shining armor to come and rescue me. She keeps pointing out that no one will ring my doorbell one day and say, "Let me take you away from this." It won't happen.

The least likely person to take on the role of white knight is your husband. He will be busy taking care of himself, especially if he is involved with legal hassles, protective services and/or therapeutic recovery programs. He will only take care of you if it fits his needs and meets his goals.

> Elaine could not believe that Matty was being so helpful. He would come back over to the house on the weekends to fix the leaking sink, and replace the oil in the car. He sent her flowers for Valentine's Day, and took her out for dinner at the club, just like they used to do every Saturday night.
>
> Only later did she realize that he mentioned the flowers to all their old friends they saw at the club, and that he was publicly more charming than usual. When she asked him to take care of a minor mix-up with one of their credit cards, he was back to his old self-centered self.

Matty was Mr. Nice Guy in front of the kids, or in front of his friends. But when it was just the two of them, he reverted to his self-centered self. He needed others to see him as a victim also, not the monster Elaine had made him out to be.

He Needs to Be Accountable for What He Did

Letting go and forgiving lets you put the responsibility back on the person who did the deed rather than continuing to assume responsibility for everything that happened. Most spouses of child molesters feel both ashamed and responsible for the actions of their husbands. It is essential to acknowledge and recognize it was *your husband* that did these terrible things, not you. It is *he* that must take the responsibility for them not you. An important part of forgiveness is holding him accountable.

FORGIVING HIM FOR WHAT HE DID TO YOU

What you are forgiving is what he did to you. You're not forgiving what he did to other people, how he may have hurt his family—his parents, his brothers, his sisters—or how he may have hurt the children he was involved with. If your spouse has been active in community affairs or taken a community leadership position, you'll also be hurt by people who felt that he betrayed the public trust. But it's important to remember that your forgiveness only applies to his hurting you, and that your forgiveness cannot cover the other people that were affected by his actions.

> Bob was an outgoing and fun-loving teenager who enjoyed working with the Sunday school classes at his church and day-care classes in his community youth groups. He had spent the summers of his high school and college years camp counseling in the nearby mountains.
>
> After graduating from college and moving to a city some thousand miles away from his hometown, Bob became very involved in an organization of adults who befriended fatherless children. He rose to positions of responsibility and respect in the organization. When he fell under investigation by the police department and was eventually arrested for child molesting, not only were his family, friends, the children that he had befriended, and the children's parents hurt by his behavior, but the larger network of friends and rela-

tionships that he had developed as a leader in the community organization as well.

Each of the people who had been hurt and betrayed by Bob's behavior needed to heal and go through a separate process of forgiveness.

Forgiveness does not mean it was okay for the person to do what he did, or that he doesn't have to face the consequences for doing it. Forgiveness does not mean simply saying, "That's okay" when he apologizes or tells you he's sorry, particularly with child molesters who have a long history of repetitive, compulsive behavior.

There may come the day when you can forgive him, but it will not come soon and it will not come easily. Forgiveness is one of the last steps, not the first step, of the recovery process. It is important not to be pressured by friends, family members, ministers, priests, or the molester himself into forgiving him.

If you try to forgive someone before you are ready to, you will find that there is still so much anger and feelings of distrust and resentment that continue to mask your feelings On the other hand, don't wait to begin your own recovery until you can forgive. What I found with many treatment program participants is that you have to forgive before you can finish, but not before you start, the recovery process.

DON'T TRY TO TEACH A PIG TO SING

The forgiveness process focuses on forgiving the bad or hurtful things that people do, rather than forgiving them for being who and what they are.

Trying to forgive somebody for who he is reminds me of one of my favorite posters that I always had in my clinical treatment room. It was a picture of a disgustingly fat, filthy, ugly old pig sitting in the middle of a mud pile. The caption to the poster said, "Don't try to teach a pig to sing—you will fail and it annoys the pig." Trying to forgive somebody for being who he is is like trying to teach a pig to sing. You're going to fail and it annoys the pig.

There is no question that child molesters are difficult, awful, reprehensible people to live with. And they have a tendency to hurt everyone around them, particularly the people they're married to. Often you will offer your help or attempt to make things better only to find out that your efforts are spurned, the need for help is denied, or even the existence of a problem is denied. It's easy to feel guilty, that somehow it's all your fault. It's like we want the molesters to be different than who they are. We expect them to be who we want them to be.

It's very difficult not to have expectations for another person, particularly if that person is someone whom you've loved and lived with for a number of years. When most of us got married and made the commitment to spend our lives with another person, we had an idea of what our rules and expectations were going to be for that relationship. We expected commitment, trust, respect, monogamy, and, above all else, the other person not to be cruel and hurtful. It's very difficult to give up our expectations. We want our spouse to keep being the person that we thought he was, rather than the person he is.

We go through major denial and disillusion as we attempt to reconcile what we want and what, in fact, we may have had in the earlier years of our relationship with the person that we are now living with. It is not uncommon to respond with the cry that you don't know who your husband is as one woman did when she found out that her husband of twenty plus years had been molesting neighborhood children. She went on to say that she felt as if she were sleeping with a man she didn't know, a stranger who had so masked who and what he was that she had no way of knowing or understanding what he had done, or who he really was.

Forgiveness is not the solution or the cure for the pain that comes when the other person is not what we want him to be. Or as Lewis Smedes says in his book *Forgiving and Forgetting*:

> *Forgiveness cannot heal our narcissistic resentments toward people for not being all that we expect them to be. Nobody can really forgive people for being what they are. Forgiveness wasn't invented for such unfair maneuvering.*

We can forgive people for the specific acts they have committed toward us, but not for being child molesters.

As Smedes goes on to say, "We overload the circuits of forgiveness when we try to forgive people for being burdens to our existence, or for not being the sort of people we want them to be." Forgiveness is not the cure for that type of hurt. When we attempt to forgive others for what they are, we not only fail, but we increase our resentments toward them because of our own failure. We end up feeling sorrier and more frustrated than before. It is also easy to feel really bad about yourself because you think, What's the matter with me? I can't even forgive someone the way I'm supposed to!

He May Not Want to Be Forgiven

You need to remember that many child molesters are in denial about their behavior. They may either deny that they have done anything or deny that anything they did do was wrong. Forgiveness is not something that they are looking for or feel they need. They have no understanding of or feel little responsibility for the impact their behavior has on people around them. And, in fact, they may get angry and/or lash out at those people who attempt to forgive or ask for understanding.

How Do You Forgive?

Many people look to spiritual advisors as experts in forgiveness. People want to follow the models their leaders have given. While this may be a good place to start, let me warn you again: Forgiveness is a very personal process. The model that is presented to you may work well for you and, then again, it may not. Don't be afraid to modify the forgiveness process and select those aspects of forgiveness models that fit for you, disregarding the ones you find either too difficult, demeaning, or trivial to fit your needs. But, don't be too quick to throw something out or to disregard a portion of somebody else's model for forgiveness just because you find it difficult or unpleasant. Forgiveness is both difficult and unpleasant at times. It may well be that the difficult task or unpleasant tool or technique is the very one that will be most helpful.

Here is a difference between being pleasant and being effective: You are looking for an effective, not necessarily a pleasant, tool.

Most of the models for forgiveness have several steps that a person goes through as he or she lets go of the bonds of a previous hurt or difficulty. There is some disagreement over how far a person needs to go and how much work needs to be done before the forgiveness can be called complete.

Most theorists suggest that after an initial time of hurt, there are four steps to forgiveness:

1. Anger
2. Hatred and betrayal
3. Reframing
4. Reconciliation

There are some theorists who suggest that the forgiveness process is incomplete unless and until you can have a reconciliation and a renewal of the relationship to its previous level. Others say that in many cases this may not be possible or even preferable.

Time to Hurt

Hurting is not a step in the forgiveness process, but the prerequisite to forgiveness. If you didn't hurt there would be nothing to forgive the other person for. Forgiving is not given for the trivial inconveniences of modern, everyday living. Forgiveness is not needed when someone bumps into you at the checkout counter at the grocery store or makes an offhand comment that you might find unpleasant or inappropriate. In these cases, an apology is in order. The apology is given, accepted, and life goes on.

Forgiveness is needed for the deep hurts that we experience, particularly those that are the result of another person's behavior. And, it has to hurt. You have to feel the pain of the wound. Denying it is there, pretending it doesn't hurt, or excusing the person who did it, not only does not resolve the hurt, but stands in the way of getting to resolution.

This does not mean that we all avoid an initial period of denial and disbelief when a crisis occurs or a wound is suffered. Our initial reaction almost always is one of shock and disbelief. We're not talking about initial reactions. What we are talking about is an acknowledgment at an emotional level that the behavior of the other person has wounded you deeply.

> Diandra was shocked when she found out that her husband had been molesting their daughter and, in fact, had intercourse with her. A simple woman, with no education and no job skills, she looks back on the situation now as something that seemed like a bad dream. Being too embarrassed and ashamed to tell anybody about what was going on, unable to see herself making it on her own, and afraid of her husband, she attempted to put it out of her mind and to deny the significance of what he did.
>
> Shortly after Diandra found out about her husband and her daughter, her daughter ran away with her boyfriend. Many years later, Diandra's daughter moved back near her parents with her own two daughters. With few job skills herself, she was only able to find part-time work and was very dependent upon her parents for financial support. The children stayed at her parents' house a good deal of the time while Diandra baby-sat. To Diandra's horror, the pattern started all over again, with her husband now starting to molest her teenage granddaughter and even make advances toward the five-year-old.
>
> When a support group member asked Diandra how she could have forgiven her husband for what he did to their daughter, she replied that she never had forgiven him. She never had sexual relations since that time and had spent thirty years being angry at him. She said she tried to convince herself that what her husband did had not had an impact and effect on their daughter. Only later could she clearly see how it not only had an effect on their daughter, but on their grandchildren as well.

Even though her daughter's molestation had happened some thirty years before with her daughter, Diandra was still not ready or able to forgive her husband for what he did. She was still very caught up in the hurt and anger of the situation. Now her pain was compounded by his having done it again, this time hurting their grandchildren.

Denying that a situation has occurred or that it has been hurtful and damaging only prolongs the hurt and prevents the situation from being resolved. It keeps you in a position of victimization.

Anger

Anger is one of the most universal reactions to discovering someone you trust and love has betrayed you in this most grievous way. The only women I have talked with who do not admit to hating their spouses for what they did are women, like Diandra, who are attempting to deny either what their spouses did, or the impact of what they did. Feeling bad, angry, and vengeful are the most typical and understandable feelings to experience not just when you first find out what he did, but as you work through the situation. It may well come back over and over again.

If you don't get in touch with your anger, or if you try to cover it with sadness or depression, it will be impossible to work through it and to release yourself from its grip.

Lots of women cover their anger with depression, or feeling sad, rather than feeling mad about what happened to them. Being depressed can be a way of staying stuck. Depression is often defined as anger directed inward rather than anger directed outward.

If you don't express your anger at the person who hurt you but instead get angry at yourself for being hurt, you're going to continue being stuck. Being the spouse of a child molester will take over and run your life, until and unless you can be angry at the person who did it rather than being angry at yourself for having had it done to you. This does not mean that you can't feel depressed, just don't stay in your depression.

Hatred and Betrayal

Hatred personalizes anger. Not only are you angry at what happened but you hate the person who did it. For spouses of child molesters the hatred they feel can be overwhelming, their hatred is the passion of their anger, and filled with visions of vengeance, revenge, and hurting the person they hate.

We only hate people we care about. We can be angry at a stranger for hurting us, and may even want to punish him or seek revenge. But we don't hate the person. We hate people we love when they have hurt us. We personalize the injury because they didn't just hurt anyone, they injured someone they were supposed to be loving toward.

Hatred is not the opposite of love. When we love someone we are bound to the person. Hatred has those same bindings. We keep the connection, only fill it with ill will rather than good will. Only when we let go and indifference overcomes hatred are the bonds broken and we are free of the other person.

Betrayal is fueled by the belief that not only did the other person do something wrong to us, but he did it in a very personal way, and broke the trust or agreement we had on how we should treat one another. In every relationship, but especially in marriage, we develop patterns of relating to one another based on spoken and unspoken rules of the relationship. These rules develop over time and are based on what we have learned a relationship should be, what we feel a relationship could be, and what we expect from one another. They form the contract governing day-to-day behavior within a relationship. They provide the moral guidelines for what we have decided together is right and wrong, moral and immoral within our relationship.

Child molesting violates those moral rules on two levels. The first level is the behavior itself. Not only is the molester sexual with someone besides his spouse, but that someone is a child. As if that isn't bad enough, the second level of betrayal is that of lying about what he did. Not only did he change the rules that bound his relationship with his spouse, but denied he did it. His lies to his wife harm the relationship more than his behavior. Trust is broken and, with it, the relationship. He has put himself, what he does, and what he wants above the agreements they had. The spouse of a molester has no way of knowing what else her husband is lying about, what other rules he has broken, and if and when he will break them again. The relationship will never be the same again.

Reframing

Reframing is the core process in forgiveness. Reframing allows you to make the shift from feeling bad about a situation to being able to forgive. Reframing takes a situation out of one mental framework and places it in another. The new framework still fits the situation. In fact, it usually fits it even better. You don't change the facts of the situation, just the perspective from which you view the facts. With this different view, it's possible to see new resolutions and actually change the outcome.

Reframing begins with an acknowledgment or admission of your ignorance. There is something that you did not know. The second step involves taking responsibility for your ignorance and the actions you took when you didn't know all that was going on. By taking responsibility for what you did, you also acknowledge your faith in your ability to change. By looking at an experience from this perspective, without blame or upset, you will be able to see alternative explanations and understandings.

Reframing lets you move to a more affirming posture for yourself, without insisting others need to change. To reframe your relationship with your molesting husband, you acknowledge that you were ignorant, that you didn't know what he was doing, and now you do. You admit to yourself that you are his wife, that no one is forcing you to stay or to take responsibility for him. You acknowledge that since you chose to believe this way, you can choose to believe a new way. It is possible to change your beliefs and take action based on your new beliefs.

When you start to reframe a situation, you develop new rules for yourself. You can judge what is right for you. You can take charge of your own life.

To effectively reframe a situation that you are stuck in—or with a person who has wronged you—you must go below the surface and let go of feelings and expectations, both for yourself and the other person. To change yourself and your perspective, it is necessary to examine the secondary gains that you get from the situation.

Secondary gains are the hidden benefits from being in an unpleasant situation. Even the worst of circumstances can have benefits. If you get rid of the negatives, you also will have to give up the positives. Not being married means you won't have to put up with his behavior, but it also means you won't share his paycheck. This is the dilemma Sheila (chapter 4) was experiencing when she considered not reporting her incesting husband. She was faced with stopping the negative, his abuse, but also with losing his retirement benefits when he was jailed. Only by getting clear with the secondary gains of an unhealthy situation can you develop a new way of looking at your life.

Reframing situations with others involves letting go: letting go of the belief that they must be who we think they should be, and accepting them for just who they are. It is difficult to understand why a person would be hurtful, especially to someone like us. It may be because the person is ignorant, and he truly has no idea of the impact or the meaning of his behavior. The response to ignorance is to give enough feedback and information, so that the situation will not happen again.

Or it may well be that the hurtful person has been so hurt himself, he is lashing out at everyone. When trying to make sense of a person like this, understanding more of what he has been through enables you to be more accepting of his behavior—recognizing he is doing the best he can—and that what he is doing has nothing to do with you. He would be the same way with anyone.

But it does not mean that you have to put up with the unpleasant behavior. It is possible, self-esteem-enhancing, and appropriate to put limits on the destructive and abusive behavior of another.

In fact, it is important not to get hooked into believing the other person's con. When he continues to behave in an unacceptable manner, and you believe him as he tries to convince you that he is different this time, then the one to confront is yourself. What is going on for you, that you believed him again this time? Usually it is that unrealistic hope that he will change, or already has. When you have a history with a difficult person, go slowly in new behavior patterns. Trust yourself, rather than the other, as he starts to make changes.

Saying "I Forgive You" and Feeling It

Oh, those words are so hard to say. It's impossible to say them when you're initially hurt. It's impossible to say them when you're in the midst of hate and anger and depression, and, yet, there comes the day when you have to say them. Not for him, but for you. Not for your children, but for yourself. Not for the other victims, but for you.

The first step in being able to say the words "I forgive" is to consider the possibility of forgiving. Ask yourself what forgiving would do for you and for the other person. When you're feeling full of hurt and full of hate, even the possibility of forgiving isn't available and, yet, as you start to move through the forgiveness process, start to consider what your life would be like if you forgive.

Forgiving means that you need to detach the action that the person did from who and what the person is. By detaching the deed from the person and forgiving him of the act, you can see that the person is frail, limited, and blemished and not the perfect person that you thought him to be, or wanted him to be. You start seeing the person as he is rather than some perfect image of who he could be or should be. Forgiving at some point involves getting into the other person's shoes and seeing him as a human being rather than just the behavior or the hurt that he has done to you.

Theologian Steven Levine, in *Healing into Life and Death*, talks about a traditional manner of practicing forgiveness. He describes it as first extending it to someone you have a resentment against and touching him with the possibility of forgiveness. You then try to picture another person who is unforgiving toward you and reach out with an openness for forgiving and a willingness to let go of the unfinished business between the two of you.

Levine's third step involves extending forgiveness to yourself. He suggests working with these steps as a meditation on a daily basis, allowing the healing to fulfill you. He suggests that asking for forgiveness and offering forgiveness is not done because of the wrongdoings, but because you no longer wish to carry the load of resentments and guilts. He suggests it allows the mind to just sink into the heart and let go and get on with it. It becomes a process of healing the hurts that you feel in your heart. Forgiveness in this way diffuses the pain and the anguish and takes the power of the hurt away from the other person and allows you to reclaim the integrity of your own life.

No longer are you defining yourself at the mercy of the crimes that your husband committed, but you see yourself as an independent person in your own right. Forgiveness allows you to reestablish boundaries between who and what you are and who and what he is.

Reconciliation

Forgiveness and reconciliation are different. Forgiveness is letting go of the hurts and resentments you've been carrying. Reconciliation is reestablishing the relationship, bringing it back to what it had been before the hurts. There are some who say there is no forgiveness without reconciliation, others who say that reconciliation, while it might be nice, is not necessary for forgiveness. And, in fact, there are some situations in which reconciliation is impossible. If the person that has caused you so much pain is dead or his whereabouts are unknown, it is impossible to go back and find him and reestablish a relationship. On the other hand, there may have been changes in your life and his life that have made the reestablishment of the former relationship impossible. Or unwise.

> Donna separated from her husband shortly after she discovered he had been molesting neighborhood children. Although he was never charged or convicted of any crimes, and continued to deny that he had done wrong, she filed for divorce and eventually moved to another town. He quickly remarried a woman who was as convinced as he was that he had done nothing wrong. Folks were just picking on him.
>
> Eventually, as Donna was able to start healing and put her own life back together, she came to a feeling of forgive-

ness and was urged to make a reconciliation by her spiritual advisor. Her advisor's position was that she would not fully experience forgiveness until she had reconciled with her former husband. Donna thought long and hard about the possibility of reconciliation and then discarded it, both because he was now married to someone else, but more importantly because he was still denying the fact that he had ever done anything wrong in the first place.

Donna still says that she's surprised that she was ever able to forgive him, and when she looks back on the forgiveness process, says that it was not something that happened in a moment but something that happened over a much longer period of time. She also says that she has no conscious awareness of when the day came that she forgave him, but that she was only aware of the forgiveness by looking back and realizing that she had changed how she felt about him, about her, and about her life.

Donna believes going back to her ex-husband while he still denies that he has done anything wrong, would be to deny her own integrity. She knows that his behavior has caused pain not only to herself, but to many children, and that to attempt a reconciliation would be to deny his dishonesty and maladjusted behavior. She says that she has spent so many years denying and fudging and avoiding reality that it is essential to her own mental health and well-being that she no longer do that. She needs to be as honest and truthful about what has happened to her as she can be. She no longer accepts his view of reality, but instead focuses on what she knows to be true.

Donna struggles with a problem many spouses of child molesters have: their molesting spouses do not admit to what they're doing or do not admit they are doing anything that needs forgiving. It is essential not to wait for them or for their permission to go through a forgiveness process. The forgiveness that you do is for you, not for him.

What Forgiveness Isn't

FORGIVENESS IS NOT EXCUSING BEHAVIOR. Forgiveness may include understanding why someone did what he did, but it doesn't mean that you have to excuse what the person did.

UNDERSTANDING WHY SOMEONE DOES SOMETHING DOESN'T MEAN THAT YOU EXCUSE THE PERSON FOR DOING IT. We can understand the feelings and we can understand the background of an individual, but that doesn't make the current behavior okay. Adults have the responsibility to control their behavior. Just because they feel like doing something doesn't mean that they have to do or are excused when they do it.

FORGIVING IS NOT FORGETTING. If you forgot about what happened, you wouldn't have to forgive. Forgiving is for those situations and experiences that continue to chew away at us. It does not mean that it never happened or that it won't happen again.

> Allison was heartsick when she realized that a neighbor had molested her son. A deeply religious woman, she prayed she would find it in her heart to forgive him and eventually started to feel a sense of forgiveness for him, and what he had done to her child.
>
> At the same time, the molester had joined a congregation similar to her own. It practiced a fundamental confession and salvation doctrine. Shortly after she started to feel some sense of forgiveness toward him, he approached her and asked for her forgiveness and begged her to pray with him. She said later that it was a relief for her to know that he had found a savior and that his life had turned around.
>
> Within six months, the man who had molested her son again started to spend more time with the child. Thinking that he had a religious conversion and was no longer a danger, she allowed the relationship to not only continue but escalate. Her sense of betrayal doubled when she discovered that the molesting had not stopped, instead escalated.

Allison's frustration and sadness stemmed from the fact that she had forgiven him and then forgotten who and what he was. She had forgiven his acts and then was fooled into believing that he now, somehow, was not the way that he used to be. You can forgive, but you shouldn't forget. Not with child molesters.

FORGIVING IS NOT CONDONING THE BEHAVIOR, NOR DOES IT MEAN THAT YOU HAVE TO TOLERATE IT. Just because you can understand or forgive somebody for something that he's done does not mean that you need to provide him with the opportunity to do it again or to not hold him accountable for what he has done.

ACCOUNTABILITY IS BOTH SPIRITUAL AND CIVIL. Even though a person, such as the man who molested Allison's child, may have experienced spiritual forgiveness, that does not mean the need for civil accounting for his behavior is erased. The forgiveness may come through a spiritual avenue but the legal and criminal aspects of the case still need to be carried out. This is one of those situations where saying "I'm sorry" is not enough.

FORGIVENESS DOES NOT MEAN THAT WHAT WAS DONE WILL BE UNDONE. An apology cannot undo what has been done. You will still have to deal with all of the legal, logistical, and social services issues. It may be that the legal and medical bills have bankrupted your family. These are the everyday consequences of a situation that cannot be erased by the forgiveness.

IF HE ASKS FOR FORGIVENESS

The question always comes up. If you forgive someone or if he asks for forgiveness, should you "take him back"? Should you "continue the relationship"? As mentioned above, there may be circumstances that prevent your relationship from coming to a full reconciliation. He or you may have remarried. He may be in jail. Even if the logistics are right, you still need to look clearly at what has happened and what expectation you have for a future relationship.

If he asks for forgiveness, it is absolutely essential that he acknowledge and understand the depth of the pain and the hurt that you have experienced, and his responsibility for that hurt. There is a dramatic difference between a request for forgiveness that discounts or denies that he has done anything wrong, and that is being asked so he can get on with life as usual, and a request for forgiveness where there is an honest and open acknowledgment of the pain he has caused.

If he asks for forgiveness, he also needs to honestly acknowledge that this is something he did, not something you did. By acknowledging both the hurt and the hate, he starts to accept responsibility for his role in causing your pain. You may well find him willing to acknowledge his responsibility for the hurt and the anger and forgive him for what he has done, and then you can consider re-establishing or continuing your relationship.

Just because you have forgiven him doesn't necessarily mean that you have to stick around and maintain the relationship. Maintaining the relationship is dependent upon having a clear promise that the situation will not happen again. You must see him, and he must see himself, as able to fulfill that promise. Here is the sticky point for most child molesters: They will promise anything to keep you there, with no ability to honor the promise.

I am not so sure that this can even be classified as "lying" to you. I think, for many child molesters, what they promise is what you want to hear rather than what they can realistically do. At the moment of the promise, they may well have some intentions or some wishful thinking that they'll be able to do what they say that they're going to do. And as soon as you turn to leave, they'll be back to business as usual.

The old childhood taunt of "Fool me once, shame on you; fool me twice, shame on me" applies here. When we allow people to continue to promise and break those promises, then we need to hold ourselves accountable. We must be accountable not for their broken promises, but for continuing to believe them when they don't tell the truth.

It becomes a matter of trust, trusting yourself to know who and what this other person is.

In the years after our divorce, when my son and I were living across the country from his father, my ex-husband would often make promises about what he would do for our son. At first, I believed him and expected him to fulfill his promises. And then as each promise didn't come to pass, it became very evident to me that what he was promising was what he *wanted* to be able to do rather than what he was actually *capable* of doing.

He continued to make promises up until shortly before he died. I learned to trust him with his promises. What I trusted was that at the time that he made a promise, he wanted it to be true. And I trusted myself to know his promises were not going to be carried out. To continue to act as if they would actually happen when I knew in my heart of hearts that he wouldn't be able to fulfill them, would be to deny my reality and hook me back into my wishful thinking that he was the person I wanted him to be, rather than the person I knew he was.

FORGIVING YOURSELF

If you think it is hard to forgive somebody else, try forgiving yourself. We can always find plenty to feel guilty about and shameful of . . . we can feel guilty for not being able to fix "it" whatever "it" is, guilty for not having done more about the situation, guilty for not having known about the situation, and guilty that children were hurt and we could not prevent it. We also can feel guilty for not being perfect and doing what the textbooks say we should do in response to this horrific crisis.

We have so much we can slip into feeling guilty about that it is not surprising that many spouses of child molesters cannot see a way out of the guilt.

One of the issues that I had to deal with the most was forgiving myself for believing him when he lied to me. Now I know that my husband was sneaky, a liar, and covered up his behavior. He, like other child molesters, knew on some level that it would shatter his life if it became public knowledge. So he lied, to me and many other people, to keep his secret.

Perhaps I felt guilty because I believed his lies. I was so sure that as a "trained professional" I could size people up and know whether or not they were telling me the truth. When I got pulled into his lies and fantasies, it was as much a blow to my own ego and my own definition of self, as it was feeling angry and frustrated at him. I evaluated and judged myself and found myself wanting.

And this takes me to the whole reason for forgiveness. While concentrating on hating him for how he ruined my life and hating myself for having such poor judgment, I could not believe in myself and my abilities to deal with the world. I had to take a realistic view, a view that included blaming my husband for his behavior, acknowledging that he had betrayed me, acknowledging that I had bad judgment in believing his lies, acknowledging that I couldn't "cure" him, or change him, and acknowledging that I could be married to a child molester.

Facing this reality hurt. It hurt even more because I had believed that it couldn't happen to me. It hurt even more because I was a trained professional, and I had been fooled. Throughout this process, I learned two lessons about forgiveness. First, you have to start forgiving before you can start to move on. You can't take action to change a situation unless and until you are ready to let go of what has happened. The second lesson that I learned is that you can't wait until you finish forgiving to take action, whether it is forgiving your spouse for what he did to you or forgiving yourself for having been deceived. Forgiving takes a long time. It is a continual process, not an event that suddenly occurs.

Part III

Practical Solutions

Chapter 10

Moving On

I know of no more encouraging fact than the unquestionable ability of man to elevate his life by conscious endeavor.

— HENRY DAVID THOREAU, American writer

For me, the first step in getting on with my life occurred the day I realized my ex-husband would not change and that there was nothing I could do about him or what he did. I could only do what I needed to do for myself. That was the day I told myself the truth about him, about what he did, and about what I could do about it all. Telling myself the truth was a hard thing to do. And it was the beginning of my journey, not the end. I had to regain my power, recognize that I did have choices about what I did and could do, and let go of him and of my identification as a victim of his behavior. As I started to regain my strength, I started to take action, started to move on and make my life the way I wanted it to be, rather than continue to define myself as a part of him and his life. The actions I took reflected the purpose and meaning of my life.

Taking action means living your life on purpose, deciding who and what you are and then choosing to live your life consistent with who you are. It means setting goals for yourself and achieving them. It means staying motivated during the rough times, when things aren't going well, when there have been difficulties, and when you don't feel like doing anything but pulling the covers over your head and turning the electric blanket up to nine.

DEFINING YOUR PURPOSE

Every life has purpose and meaning. Even when it seems as if your life has no direction or focus, the purpose of your life forms the base of your life. For spouses of child molesters, like other people who have been victimized, it is easy to drift, to lose focus, or to only see the trauma. From here is a short step to accepting the label of victim as the definition of your life.

> *Joyce fell into this trap after she was brutally raped. A social worker, she had been working the late shift in a children's shelter in a large metropolitan suburb. She took the bus home each night, and walked the remaining two blocks to her apartment.*
>
> *She said the night she was raped was like every other night until a stranger came out of the alley and grabbed her. He was never caught.*
>
> *Now, three years later, she still isn't working steadily, won't leave her apartment after dark, and wears loose, bulky clothes with long sleeves and high necks, even in the summer. She doesn't want to provoke anyone else to take advantage of her.*

Joyce has allowed her rape to define her life. The purpose she now sees is avoiding further assaults. She is still seeing herself only as a victim. You can fall into the same trap if you only see yourself as the spouse of a child molester.

Finding the meaning in your life means knowing in what direction you want to go. It is the difference between letting your life happen, making it happen, and trying to force it to happen. In defining your life's meaning, drifting and forcing don't work. Making your life happen *does* work.

Uncovering your life's purpose can be very confusing because it involves a lot of paradox. You will be faced with the paradoxes that you have been living:

- Other people (like your husband) control your life.
- What happened was so awful no good can come of it.
- You have no choices that count.
- You have to _____ (fill in the blank).

To move on, to make a better life for your yourself, you need to resolve each paradox, face the truth, make choices, and see yourself as empowered. You need to take action.

Defining your purpose is a balancing act: between the specific and the general, the inspiring and the attainable. It both reflects the world you live in and transforms your world into something new. Purpose is lived in the details of daily behavior, and provides structure for the overall plan of your life. Stating your purpose helps keep you focused and flexible at the same time, reflecting the changes you experience as you grow, as well as the changes other people and circumstances bring into your life.

Defining the meaning in your life is an activity that takes time. You can't hurry the process. You need time to discover and uncover the purpose and meaning of your life.

Specific and General

Purpose defines the criteria for daily behavioral choices and life decisions. If a part of your purpose is to live a healthy, fit lifestyle, not smoking and eating a low-fat diet are givens, not decisions. Not only is the purpose you embrace reflected in the specific actions that you take, but it determines them. As you shift to a new focus in your life, you will stop doing things that used to fit, but don't anymore. Those old behaviors aren't like you anymore. You will soon find that activities or actions that you might have struggled with in the past are not only easier, but second nature.

Lofty and Inspiring

The meaning of your life challenges you to bigger and better accomplishments. It will be a stretch, which may never be accomplished. There will always be new challenges.

When you were in the survival mode, just getting through each day was a big enough challenge. Now, your purpose and meaning move beyond yourself. No longer are you the center of the universe, but an embarkation point into the universe.

Even though you may never fully achieve your life purpose, it doesn't mean you shouldn't have one. Life purpose sets the direction and the challenge; it does not demand achieving every objective. When you've accomplished all there is for you to accomplish, you die. Having more to do, or you feel called to do, means your life isn't over yet.

Reasonable, Not Limiting

Meaning and purpose in life must make sense in the reality of the world you live in. It is difficult to talk about making sense and being reasonable without sounding like I am suggesting you limit your aspirations. The key is to find a way to live the way you see as important, without being dependent on a single way of expressing that need.

After I started feeling better about myself, I realized part of the good that could come from my experience involved reaching out and helping other women who were going through what I had gone through. I started talking to other professionals about referrals, gave numerous informational presentations and newspaper interviews. And new clients started coming, first for initial interviews, and then for support groups or individual therapy. I was heartened by the response.

Then the pressures started to build. There were several spouses of child molesters who wanted me to help them help their spouses. The men wouldn't consider treatment and wouldn't change. They felt they just needed to be more forgiving and open and their problems would be resolved.

A pastor said he certainly didn't have these problems in his congregation. The men were Christians, after all. He didn't want to hear about the pastors' wives and children I had met who had been abused by the Christian men of the cloth. A therapist said the bulk of his practice was child molesters and all their wives wanted to stand by their men. He found it hard to believe any woman would consider leaving her molesting husband. Needless to say, no referrals came from either this pastor or this therapist. But I knew there were women who needed help for themselves. I wanted to put the focus on the women who had been victims: not the children, not the men.

Although I continued treating other women who had been spouses of child molesters, I realized that I wanted to do more, to reach a wider audience. I could have returned to an academic environment where I could do research on the causes or the conditions of this experience. I could have opened a clinic where I could train other therapists to use some of the treatment methods I had developed. Either would have meant I could have developed an academic reputation and delivered papers to conferences from the perspective of a professional in the field. But, that didn't fit for me. I didn't want to go back to a campus. And, I didn't want to take on the role of the disinterested professional. What I wanted was to reassure other women that they had been victimized and that they could make a difference in their own lives. I could only do that by telling my story.

Telling my story was both a challenge and a comfort. The challenge was actually writing a real book, as it looked to be a huge task. I had stopped myself before because I was afraid I wasn't up to the task. I had limited myself. The comfort came from trusting my experience. I had become the expert on me. I knew my material. So I worked to make the challenge reasonable. I chose the task that I knew would be hard, but that I knew I could do.

Lived in the Details

Purpose and meaning is lived in the details. It is visible in the small things you do on a daily basis as well as major life decisions. Knowing what you stand for, and stand on, gives a solid base for life action. It prepares you for the future, while honoring the past.

Defining your life holds you accountable for acting accordingly. It provides the daily bench marks against which you can assess your behavior. It provides the guidelines for self-control and discipline. If you decide to focus on the future, and then find yourself telling one more stranger what a skunk your now ex-husband is, you've slipped back into old patterns. Setting a new purpose means acting as if your purpose is already well-formed.

The Master Paradox

Stating your purpose puts you in touch with what management consultant Tom Peters calls the master paradox: staying focused and flexible at the same time. Not having enough focus means you can be tossed about by each new idea and opportunity. Not having enough flexibility means you can be caught in a project or plan that is no longer working. The key is to balance focus and flexibility.

You need to be focused enough to carry to completion projects that fit your purpose, while staying flexible enough to make the changes that allow you to take advantage of unforeseen opportunities, or to make the necessary adjustments to projects that aren't working out as anticipated. Being too focused is as self-defeating as being too flexible. Typically, people feel most comfortable with either focus or flexibility, and then approach each project in their favorite way. Focus and flexibility become ingrained styles. Having to work with someone who approaches his or her work differently than you do also can be frustrating. Focused people demand that their more flexible colleagues put some structure in their work. The flexible folks respond by suggesting that their focused co-workers loosen up. To be most effective, flexibility and focus are both necessary. Finding the balance between the two is key.

Life is a temporary assignment. Even when you define your purpose and develop a life plan, it is likely your life won't turn out exactly the way you planned it. Some people use this as a reason not to plan. Why bother planning, if there is no guarantee my plan will happen? Don't fall into this trap. Even with the best of plans, it is impossible to cover and account for all contingencies. Even if you can't be guaranteed your plans will come out the way you anticipate, you still need to plan. If you don't plan, you can be sure your life won't be what you wanted.

SETTING GOALS

Setting goals is what lets you translate your purpose into action. It is the base for planning. But. lots of people have trouble setting and achieving goals. This is particularly true for people who have been letting other people define their lives. If you have been a person to whom things happen, rather than someone who makes things happen, you probably could use a refresher course on setting goals. When you don't use a skill for some time, you forget how to do it, or even that you ever knew how to do it. Goal-setting is a skill, not a secret. You need to review a few basics and then practice.

Writing Effective Goal Statements

Effective goal statements answer the questions Who will do what? By when? At what cost? They don't directly answer the why question. Why? is the link back to purpose. They also don't answer the how question. How? is addressed by planning. Effective goal statements tie down the behavior timetables and the results that are desired. They address the what and when of a project. Effective goals share several characteristics:

- **They have an action verb.** Action verbs say what will happen. They are specific. If you are involving other people in your goals, make sure you all share the same definitions and assumptions about the actions you will be taking.

- **They are measurable.** They set specific targets by specific dates. If you don't have specific amounts, you can't tell if you are succeeding or not. And you can't tell if you can succeed in the time you have set for yourself.

- **They set a budget.** Every project needs some type of resources, time, money, effort. It is unreasonable to expect that you will be able to achieve your goals without some expenditures. Creating your budget establishes your priorities. You will work on and fund those projects that are most important to you.

- **They relate to your purpose.** The most motivating goals are the ones that are the most important to you. Importance is defined by how close they fit your purpose.

Sabotaging Yourself with Goal-Setting

One of the reasons that people have trouble achieving their goals is that they fall into patterns with the ways they set their goals. These patterns insure that they will be unable to achieve what they want to achieve. Check your goals for these predictable sabotages:

- **Too big:** When goals are too big they are overwhelming. They become difficult to stay with and accomplish. Break enormous goals down into manageable, smaller projects.

- **Too easy:** Goals that are too easy are seen as too trivial to bother with. Instead of just finishing a project that is easy, many people procrastinate, find it boring, or develop a "why bother" attitude. "If it's easy, it can't be important" is the attitude that sets in. But, importance is not determined by challenge, but by how it fits into the overall plan.

- **Too many:** For many people, there are just too many important, exciting, challenging things to do. There is no way that everything we want to do can be done, at least at the same time. Setting goals and developing projects means having to prioritize. Trying to do too many things, or too much of any one thing at a time, insures that something will fall off your plate. Better to focus in on a few things, and do them well and thoroughly, than to try to do too many things at the same time.

- **No ownership:** Ownership for goals is felt when the person who is responsible for implementing the project, or those people directly impacted by the project, participate in the goal-setting process. Always doing what other people want leads to feelings of anger and resentment. If you are driven by "shoulds" you will increase the scope of your resentment from one person to the way life is.

Setting goals is not a one-time activity. You also need to check and be sure your actions are supporting your goals. Whether you plan your activities in detail each day, outline general activities at the start of your week, or clean up the details at the end of the week, your daily and weekly activities need to be planned for each of your goal areas. Unless you plan for them, the activities won't happen. Review each goal area regularly. Set aside time just for yourself. I take a few minutes each Sunday night, once a quarter, and the time between Christmas and the New Year. Review each goal area:

- **Personal well-being:** Includes health and fitness goals, both physical and mental. Are you making you a priority? When did you last check in with your health care provider? Are you getting enough exercise? The right kind of food? Smoking or drinking too much?

- **Work:** What are you taking charge of? Are there activities or developmental areas that need attention?

- **Career and education:** You have to provide for yourself. What skills and knowledge do you need to build on? Is there a low-cost evening class at your local high school or community college that could help you get ahead? Is there an alternative degree program available so you can get your degree? What kind of job-training courses are available? Keeping skills and knowledge current is what ensures job security.

- **Friends and family:** There are such pressures for our time that it is easy to focus on the quality of the time you spend with others, not the quantity of time. But the fact remains, nurturing relationships with both family members and friends takes time. Time to play, time to be caring, time to be there and be supportive. Building a base during the easier times makes it more certain there will be friends and family available when a crisis occurs.

- **Financial:** When your personal finances have been destroyed, it is difficult to envision you'll ever recover. By not setting goals and making plans you won't. It is easy to put off taking charge of your finances. There is no good time to start working on financial issues. Most of us can always find more to buy or spend on than our income will cover. But, by setting even modest goals, and achieving them, you'll be on the way to solvency again.

- **Spiritual:** When your life has been severely impacted by the ill will of another, it is hard to turn your attention to spiritual matters. Many women report their faith was sorely tested, if not shattered, by what their husbands have done. Others report their faith has been damaged more by the uncaring or hostile reactions of their pastors, priests, or rabbis, as well as their fellow parishioners. Surely this is a time when the automatic, comfortable patterns of your previous spiritual life will be challenged. Whether they will be loosened or strengthened will be up to you.

PLANNING AND IMPLEMENTATION

The best goals in the world are ineffective without implementation. Implementation is the how question that translates goals into action. Each of us develops a system to fit our needs and style. For some people it is a structured list that is carefully rewritten each morning; others use a running weekly list. There is no one right way to keep track of goals and everyday activities. Often the simplest equipment can be the most effective. A simple pocket calendar and steno pad can be as effective as the most elaborate and expensive leather-bound books and software packages. The system you use to keep track of your activities isn't important. What is important is to have a system that works for you. Only by keeping track of your daily activities can you tell if you are on track with your goals. The system you use becomes your feedback system, bringing you data about what you have done.

Feedback not only lets you know when you have accomplished a task, but also if what you did got you what you wanted. Both issues need to be addressed to evaluate and modify what you have been doing. Right after I separated from my husband, before I realized that the charges against him were in fact true, I arranged my business to do a lot of work out of town. My son could stay with his father and I could make more money in less time than when I worked in town. It seemed like a good solution. But, as I realized that the charges were true, and I needed to make a life for me and for my son where I would be the only residential parent, my work activities had to change. Being out of town was no longer getting me what I wanted and what he needed. I changed the focus of the business to working for fewer clients in a specific area, rather than all over the country. Feedback, checking against the goals I had set, pointed to the changes I needed to make.

Goal statements don't have to involve large projects to have significant impact. Even small projects can reap big results. When I was still bogged down in the depression and shock of discovering what my husband had done, I had moved to a small apartment. I wasn't paying much attention to where I was living, or to the furnishings until I walked up to the door one day and realized anyone walking by could look right in the windows and see everything in the apartment. I realized I needed sheer curtains on the windows to let in the light and still give me the privacy I wanted.

I measured the windows, calculated the sizes, shopped for the curtains and the rods, and installed them. I was justly proud of myself when I finished. Although they were a bit crooked, the curtains were up and I had regained my privacy.

More importantly, I had started taking action. I had started reclaiming my life. I was no longer only wallowing in my self-pity, feeling victimized and helpless. I was no longer only caught up in the inactivity and lethargy of depression. As trivial and seemingly insignificant as putting up a set of eight-dollar curtains was, it became symbolic, liberating, and energizing.

I wish I could tell you I only went uphill from there. I didn't. There were still many days of feeling down, many more sessions with lawyers and hearings, additional young boys who came forward, identifying themselves as victims of my husband. It would be almost two more years before that day when I made a formal treatment plan for myself. But, the foundation was laid. I started more consciously choosing what I would do and with whom I would do it. I started making plans, trying new activities, challenging myself. I stopped waiting until I felt like doing something and did what I know needed to be done. I was reclaiming my power and my life.

Some of the plans I put in place were as trivial as putting up the curtains. An avid miniaturist, I found a dollhouse that I had always wanted in a shop that was closing. It was on closeout for a third of what it normally cost. I bought it in a flash and then budgeted twenty-five dollars to finish it by using mostly supplies I had on hand. For weeks it was an engrossing activity that kept my hands busy as I started to heal. It is still a prized possession.

Another prized possession is the now-tattered T-shirt with a Grand Canyon logo on the front. I had always hiked and camped with my husband. Now I joined a group of nineteen other women, ranging in age from nineteen to sixty-five, who climbed to the bottom of the Grand Canyon. I was the last one out, but I made it. As I came over the edge of the canyon, near the lodge, a couple remarked how much they were impressed that someone as out of shape, overweight, and old as myself could do something so hard. I chuckled to myself all the way home. I had accomplished something I never thought I could do.

Other plans were more significant. I actively cultivated clients on the other coast, getting ready for the day when I knew I would have to leave town. I really didn't want to leave my family and friends, and was sad when I did, but I knew I had to get both my son and myself away from the publicity, whispers, and constant reminders of what had happened. When the day for leaving came, I knew I could move my son and myself with the assurance of being able to support myself.

Even today, the tough times come. As I have been writing this book, I found myself slipping back into unpleasant feelings as I remembered and relived what I experienced. A stranger in a computer store pressed me to tell her the content of the book I was writing, and then yelled at me, shaking her finger in my face as she backed me up against a display. It was all my fault, she said. I was the cause of child abuse. I felt lucky to escape her tongue-lashing without having been physically assaulted.

I also remembered my friend who kept telling me I chose to marry a child molester, I wanted to be victimized, I had to stop seeing him as the cause of my troubles. She insisted I alone was responsible for everything that had happened. I haven't talked to her again.

I contrast those experiences with the loving relationship I have with and the support I get from the young man who is my son. And the fearful, anonymous telephone calls I get after doing a workshop or presentation. from courageous women who are trying to make sense of their lives and deal with being married to a child molester. And the support and love form my family and friends.

And I know I'm better, and the world is better, for my having told my story.

Chapter 11

First Aid Survival Kit

I don't wait for moods. You accomplish nothing if you do that. Your mind must know it has got to get down to earth.

— PEARL BUCK

Most women do not expect to find themselves in the position of being the spouse of a child molester. In fact, when most women find out the man they married, or have been with for some time, has been molesting their children or neighborhood children, they can't believe it, want to deny it, look for the magic that will allow them to take their lives back to the way it used to be.

This chapter is designed to help you when you first find out about the event, when you are trying to cope with the crises, and as you try to put your life back together. It is divided into three sections:

1. Reassurance:
   - That you are not alone
   - That you are not responsible

- That you are not crazy
- That it will someday, some way get better

2. Specific suggestions:
   - For setting up a support team
   - For maneuvering through the legal and social services systems
   - For taking care of yourself when your life is falling apart
   - For living with the stress

3. Taking the next steps:
   - Designing your own recovery program
   - Assessing the choices and resources you have
   - Self-help programs

REASSURANCE

You are not responsible for his sexual behavior. Adults are responsible for their own sexual behavior. Yet you may be blamed, you may blame yourself, you may feel guilty for causing what he did. But consider:

- You were not there.
- He made a choice to do what he did.
- Even if he was drunk, angry, or aroused, he is responsible for doing what he did and is now accountable for it.
- To some extent, you will be held legally liable for his behavior. This is not fair. Life isn't fair.

It will be difficult to sort out your feelings of guilt and shame around his behavior and the legal consequences that you experience. You are not crazy, even though you may feel like your life is totally out of control, you have no control over your feelings, and you are unable to concentrate or accomplish routine tasks. In this kind of a situation it is normal to feel awful, to cry a lot, to be agitated, to be unable to sleep, and to worry alot. It is a terrible time in a person's life.

- If you go for therapy or counseling you may be given a psychiatric diagnosis. This is for their records and to facilitate insurance payments. Do not take it as a label for life.
- Do not confuse realistic upset with "back ward" crazy.
- As bad as you feel and as dark as it looks you will feel better, usually within a period of a few months, not days, and not years.

It is not uncommon for women to isolate themselves from their family, friends, and community. For many women the feelings of shame and guilt are so overwhelming, they can't face their friends.

Feeling bad is how to feel. Don't feel bad about feeling bad.

Blaming Statements and Responses

If you are confronted with blaming statements, the following list provides you with some very straightforward and healthy responses.

Statement:	You shouldn't have told.
Possible response:	If he didn't do it, there would be nothing to tell.
Possible response:	If I hadn't told, he would still be doing it.
Statement:	If you had been more sexually available, he wouldn't have done it.
Possible response:	I am not responsible for his sexual behavior.
Statement:	The child was being seductive.
Possible response:	Adults are the responsible party. It is up to the adult to set limits.
Statement:	It was only a couple of times.
Possible response:	Even one time is too many.
Statement:	It wasn't all that bad.
Possible response:	Any sexual abuse is damaging to the victims.

Statement:	Why did he do it?
Possible response:	I don't know, you will have to ask him.
Statement:	You must have known.
Possible response:	I didn't.
Statement:	You encouraged him so you wouldn't have to have sex with him.
Possible response:	He is responsible for his behavior.
Statement:	It's the media . . . all these young girls half-clothed in ads.
Possible response:	Most men don't molest children and they see the same ads.
Possible response:	An adult is responsible for his sexual behavior.
Statement:	You should have stopped him sooner.
Possible response:	His sexual behavior is his responsibility.
Statement:	All men have these urges.
Possible response:	Most men don't molest children. There is a difference between feelings and behavior.
Statement:	If you were a good Christian you would forgive him.
Possible response:	That is between me and my God (my Higher Power).
Statement:	You must be wrong, he wouldn't.
Possible response:	The evidence shows he did.
Statement:	But he denies he did it.
Possible response:	That is what he is saying.
Statement:	The child is just making this up.
Possible response:	Young children seldom lie about these matters.
Statement:	If you hadn't been so sexually aggressive, he wouldn't have done what he did.
Possible response:	He is responsible for his sexual behavior.
Statement:	He must have been abused as a child.
Possible response:	That is irrelevant. There is no excuse for what he did.

Specific Suggestions

Getting Help
You can't do it all alone. As attractive as it may seem to not to have to rely on anyone at this point, you can't do it all yourself. You will need two kinds of support, one for sympathy, one for solutions.

Getting Sympathy
Choose two or three good friends or family members who don't blame, inflict advice, or demand action as your primary sympathy team. Make sure you have more than one or two. One person may not be available when you need someone, and spreading the action around will prevent support team burnout.

- You need to hang out and cry, beat your breast, and express your anger and anguish.

- You need the freedom to feel/be confused, frustrated, unclear, and ambivalent.

- You need to be able to express and clarify your feelings in a safe place.

Finding Solutions
Finding solutions involves assembling a support team of professionals who are experienced in dealing with the problems that you are facing.

- Choose a friend or family member who can be your administrator. You will miss deadlines, appointments, or other obligations just because you are experiencing such strong feelings so much of the time. Having an administrative support person frees you up from having to remember to remember.

- Remember the professionals you use are your employees, you pay them. They work for you. You decide if they are compatible with you, if you can work together, if they are timely, honest, and clear with you.

- Tell the truth, the whole truth, or they can't help you.

- They will not always tell you what you want to hear, but what you need to hear. Often you don't have to like it but you do need to do it or hear it.

- Keep the charter clear. Define what problems they are helping you with and which they aren't. Keep the boundaries visible. Do not let them grind their own ax with your case.

- Don't share professionals with your spouse or the other victims. You deserve your own therapist, lawyer, support groups.

- This is not the time or is it your job to train a professional in a new area of expertise. Find support professionals who are already experienced.

Support Groups

Support groups and self-help groups can offer both sympathy and solutions. They help you not feel alone, can call you on your behaviors or thinking distortions, and help you deal with the shame and guilt.

- Feel free to shop support groups to find the one that fits for you. Attend several meetings, meet for coffee afterward with some of the group members.

- Not all groups with the same affiliations are alike. Some groups have stronger cliques, others are more welcoming of newcomers. Some are more optimistic than others. Many have grown very large, others are quite small. You decide which one fits for you.

- Several 800 numbers are given in the resources section. Feel free to call for referrals, that's what they are there for.

- If you can't find a group that fits for you, start one of your own. Robin Norwood's *Women Who Love Too Much* has an excellent set of guidelines for starting and maintaining your own group.

Courts and Lawyers

One woman said watching the lawyers and the court process was like watching an old movie where they were dancing a minuet. Everyone seemed to go through their steps, doing their own thing, while she sat on the sideline ignored. It was as if she were watching an exercise in which she had no part. What she said or did was not taken into account and yet she had to listen to and adhere to the decisions that were made about her.

For people with control issues, court is a nightmare. Not only do you give up your control, you often don't even have any chance for input. In order to make the judicial process a bit less taxing, keep in mind the following points:

- There are very strict rules of procedures that must be followed or your case will be jeopardized.

- You are dependent upon your attorney to do a good job for you, being your advocate and acting in your best interests. For the most part, he or she will.

- Don't keep secrets from your attorney. You can't shock your attorney—he or she won't shame you. What your attorney doesn't know can and will hurt you.

- If you are confused about, don't understand, or don't like what is going on, do not act on your own or you will jeopardize your case. Either work through your own attorney or get a new one.

- Most attorneys think and act strategically. What may look like giving away a major point may be strategically helpful later on. Or it may look like he or she has given up on something that was important to you. If your attorney thinks he or she has lost the point, he or she may back off to avoid antagonizing the court.

- Judges put their pants on one leg at a time, just like the rest of us. Some will rely heavily on the input of others, others make all the decisions themselves. Your attorney can help you understand what type of judge you have drawn for your case.

Social Services System

In some states this is called the Department of Social Services, the Department of Protective Services, or the Department of Child Welfare. Whatever it is called, these are the people who are charged with doing the investigations, recommending removing children from homes they decide are abusive or dangerous, and, as one former DSS manager said, strengthening the American family. If that is supposed to be so, someone should point out that the system is not working.

Every spouse of a child molester has her own horror story of dealing with the social services system. You are not alone with this one. This is when the old joke of "I'm here from the government to help you" rings most hollow. If you feel out of control with the court system, the social services system will be worse for you. However, the following information may help you deal with your encounters with the system and its representatives:

- The premise under which the social services system operates is that once a report is made, the incident and the resolution of the incident is the public's responsibility, not the family's responsibility.

- What this means to you, is that once the incident becomes public, your rights and your ability to take action are severely limited by what the laws and the social services system employees determine is in the best interest of your children.

- Their "best interest" may or may not be consistent with what you, or your children, believe.

- The timing of the actions taken, who is involved, and who can not be involved are also determined by state law and social services policy.

- This is a most important time to involve your "administrator" support person. When you feel strongly, it is difficult to focus on the specific rules, regulations, deadlines, and procedures that must be adhered to. Have someone else with you to help you keep track of the details you will miss.

- Some support groups and attorneys suggest keeping notes of each contact, who was there, what was said, and what action was taken. This can offer some semblance of feeling like you have some input or control, and can help keep the details straight on the many contacts and people you will see. It also may be helpful with the legal proceedings.

Living with the Stress

> *Lord, grant me the serenity to accept the things I cannot change, the courage to change the things I can change and the wisdom to know the difference.*

The serenity prayer favored by twelve-step programs is an apt model for dealing with the stresses of the acute crisis as well as the ongoing hassles.

The courage to control the controllable applies first to recognizing choices you are making and can make. By using language that acknowledges you are making a choice, you will feel more in control and more empowered in dealing with situations and issues.

- This isn't the time . . .
- I won't deal with this now . . .
- I don't want to . . .

rather than "I can't . . ." or "I have to . . ." Even if it is a trivial event, like ordering your lunch in a restaurant, acknowledge the power of making choices.

DESIGNING YOUR OWN RECOVERY PROGRAM

Designing your own recovery program entails planning a series of steps, or experiences, that will get you the information and activities you need to make the changes you want to make. Some of the steps will be small, others more significant. Some will be no- or low-cost, others may take an investment of both time and/or money. Some you will finish in a day, others will need to be done daily. Some activities will be "prep steps," that is, activities that will prepare the way for later learnings or other activities.

Some steps will be easy and fun, others hard or unpleasant. Discomfort is one of the hallmarks of a recovery program. You will be thinking about things in new and different ways. You will be trying out new behaviors, testing your skills and abilities. I often tell seminar participants that they will probably be offended by some of the things they will hear, or by an exercise or suggestion. The offense comes because your old beliefs and feelings are being challenged. So, don't let discomfort stop you from starting to recover.

By the same token, don't let the recovery program become a new source of abuse in your life. You have to be the judge of when a program, facilitator, therapist, or other professional is right for you, and when it will be time to move on. And move on you must. A good recovery program combines a variety of experiences, new learnings, and challenges.

Get More Information

- Get more information about what has happened to you. Use the book list in the bibliography, use the bibliographies from the books or pamphlets you read.

- Get more information from other women who have experienced what you have experienced. This may mean telling more people about what has happened to you or going to a support group. Overcome your natural inclination to hide. Reach out. You need to know you aren't alone, and by having conversations with other spouses of child molesters, you will probably feel less isolated and more connected.

- The National Center for Missing and Exploited Children (listed in the Self-Help Programs and Informational Resources section) has lots of information about child molesters, their differences, and their similarities. Their information is collected in collaboration with the FBI, is based on solid research, and is not sensationalized.

- If a lack of confidence in your own competence is an issue, take noncredit class through your local high school, community college, or recreation department. Often community service agencies such as the YWCA or business and professional women's associations offer low-cost seminars or short courses. A noncredit course is great for getting the information you need while not having to deal with tests, admissions criteria, and grades.

- Use your library, or if you are concerned with privacy, go to the library in a nearby town. Libraries are safe, comfortable, quiet places where everyone leaves everyone else alone. You can read, study, or do research without being bothered. Make use of the reference librarian. He or she can show you how to use the new electronic card catalogue and periodical index, direct you to journals and articles, and orient you to the layout of the stacks and reference materials.

- Go on line. Every major on-line service (America Online, CompuServe, Prodigy) has a discussion area where you can meet others who are dealing with the same issues you are. If you have trouble finding the area, either start poking around on your own, or send your question via e-mail to the customer service representatives. They are very responsive, usually answering requests within twenty-four hours.

- If you use an on-line service be sure to protect yourself by not giving out your home address, phone number, or other identifying information to strangers. If you are flamed, or attacked, don't respond to the rude questions or report the abuse to the moderator.

- Don't shortchange yourself by using only one method to gather information. Whether you hate it or love it, relying on one program means you lose out. If you hate it, you will hesitate to keep up the work on yourself. If you love it, you may lose yourself in the program and just replace one all-encompassing issue in your life with another.

Try New Things

- Seriously consider individual counseling or therapy. Many health insurance companies cover treatment costs. If money is an issue, or if you have no insurance, consider a women's center, a community mental health agency, or low-fee, non-profit programs sponsored by religious organizations.

- Group therapy can be very beneficial, especially if the focus of the group is on your role as the spouse of a child molester, rather than as the mother of the child who was abused.

- Self-help groups and organizations can be great, or a great pain. Each group will need to be carefully evaluated (see Assessing a Self-Help Group later in this section) not only for how good they are, but for how well they fit with who you are and the issues you are dealing with.

- Different therapies, groups, self-help groups can help at different times. It will take awhile to work through your issues. Don't expect one therapist or one group to help you resolve everything.

- Most of the community resources mentioned previously that offer informational classes (YWCA, recreational departments, community colleges) also offer experiential workshops or self-help classes. They can be an excellent source for learning new skills, and also for making new friends and acquaintances.

- You can only spend so much time in therapy. Make sure you start applying what you have learned about yourself to new behaviors, new activities, and new experiences. Try a new sport, go somewhere you have never gone before, challenge yourself to take on activities you would rather avoid. If confrontation and stating your needs has been difficult for you, exchange the present you received that you didn't want, return the toaster that was defective, complain about the overcharges on your utility bill.

- Treat yourself. One client included a monthly trip to a museum opening, the theater, or a special concert in her treatment program. She said she realized she had been waiting to live her life until all her problems were over. What she started doing was living her life and solving her problems at the same time.

ASSESSING YOUR CHOICES AND RESOURCES

Assessing the competency of professional helpers is difficult when you are in pain. Yet, it is essential that you do so. I am always startled when someone calls me to set up a therapy appointment and never asks any questions about my background, training, or how I do therapy. It is your money, your time, and your life that is going to be invested in this treatment program. You are the "boss," the person who is doing the hiring. It is up to you to determine if the professional you are hiring is the right one for you.

Assessing a Therapist

Assessing a therapist means looking at the attitudes and approaches the therapist uses, as well as the logistics of the relationship. There has been much debate about whether a male or female therapist is better for women who are dealing with sexual issues. In my mind, the jury is still out. Because you need to feel comfortable with your therapist, his or her skill and sensitivity may be more important than gender. You may take the opportunity to work with both men and women, at different times, or in different settings.

When looking for a therapist, ask friends or family members who they have used and who has been helpful to them. Also, ask who they would stay away from and why. Ask your attorney, your religious advisor, or your physician for suggestions, and find out why he or she recommends that particular therapist.

When you have a name, make an exploratory appointment, or interview the person on the phone. Often, there will be no charge for an initial appointment unless the person decides to continue. Most therapists don't charge for initial, short (15 to 20 minutes) phone interviews.

Use the following questions to guide your selection process:

- Have you worked with spouses of child molesters before?
- What therapeutic approaches do you use with them?
- Have you worked with molesters?
- How do you work with them?
- If you haven't worked with spouses of child molesters before, how would you get more information about what issues are important and what approaches have been successful?
- How do you see the role of the wife of a molester vis-a-vis his behavior?
- Do you offer group as well as individual therapy? If not, would you support my attending a self-help group or therapy group while in treatment with you?
- How long do people usually stay in therapy with you?
- What is your professional background and training?
- How much do you charge? What payment arrangements do you make?

Characteristics to Look for in a Therapist

The following characteristics are found in therapists who have proven to be most effective with battered women. While the list may not fit exactly, it is a good starting point to identify someone with whom you could work. Generally, effective therapists:

- Support women who have been victimized
- Don't accept stereotyped myths about battering relationships
- Are willing to cooperate and untangle bureaucracy for unskilled clients
- Collaborate with other professionals
- Deal with their own fear of violence

- Understand how institutions oppress and reinforce women's victimization
- Are willing to be the role models for their clients
- Are willing to deal with complicated cases
- Tolerate clients' anger
- Tolerate horror stories and terrorizing events
- Allow their clients to work through their issues without pushing too fast
- Respect and believe in people's capacity to change and grow

Assessing a Self-Help Group

Self-help groups can be inexpensive, effective opportunities for confronting issues that you would rather avoid, learning more about yourself, and trying new behaviors in a safe environment. They can also support unhealthy behaviors, avoid dealing with the issues that need to be dealt with, and ostracize people for changing or getting better. Groups vary considerably, even groups that are sponsored or affiliated with the same national organization. If at all possible, visit a group before making a commitment to joining. Use that visit to assess the effectiveness of the group, your comfort level, and the fit of the group to the issues you are working on. Keep the following questions in mind as you select a group:

- What is the mission, goals, or model of approach that is used? Do people in the group realize that there is a common focus or does everyone do his or her own thing?
- What is the relationship with the national or sponsoring organization? Is this clear to the group members?
- What training or experience do the facilitators have?
- If it is a leaderless group, how do the "natural group leaders" influence and direct the workings of the group?
- What is the tone, or the atmosphere, of the group? Is confrontation and attack the order of the day or do participants

support one another without question? (Either of these approaches can be destructive and/or unhealthy. You are looking for a combination of support and confrontation, not one or the other.)

- How are new people incorporated into the group?
- How do people "graduate" and leave the group? (Beware of groups where there is no expectation of finishing and/or not needing the group in the future. You are here to deal with issues and get better, not stay stuck.)

Self-Help Programs and Informational Resources

There are few self-help programs designed specifically for women who have been married to child molesters. The following list includes groups with other primary affiliations that may prove helpful. Be sure to keep the previously mentioned cautions and assessments procedures in mind as you look for a group for yourself. Individual groups vary dramatically in adequacy, care, and effectiveness. Take care of yourself!

Parents United is designed to help families where incest has been an issue. Some women have found these groups very helpful; others felt they were being coerced into forgiving prematurely, or reuniting the family at the cost of glossing over their own feelings and issues.

P.O. Box 852
San Jose, CA 95108
(408) 280-5055

Twelve-step programs are usually listed in your local phone directory. Most will maintain an answering machine with volunteers to return your calls.

National Coalition Against Domestic Violence supports local shelters and programs for battered women and children. Local shelters are listed in the Community Assistance section of your local phone book.
1500 Massachusetts Ave., NW
Washington, D.C. 20005
(303) 839-1852

National Coalition Against Sexual Assault supports local rape crisis centers and hotlines. Local centers often provide emergency support services, therapy, and self-help groups as well as serve as a source of information about sexual abuse. Staffed by volunteers who often have been the victims of sexual assault, the fees for service are nominal or are based on a sliding scale.
P.O. Box 21378
Washington, D.C.
(202) 293-8860

The National Center for Missing and Exploited Children, in cooperation with the Federal Bureau of Investigation, has an excellent series of low-cost and free materials about child molesters, protecting your children, and how to deal with perpetrators.
2101 Wilson Blvd, Suite 550
Arlington, VA 22201-3052
(800) 843-5678 (hotline to report missing or exploited children)
(703) 235-3900 (business office)

Bibliography

I have read all of these books over and over again . . . and in the end, disagreed with some, agreed with others, and made others my handbooks for dealing with the stress and depression. Still others helped me understand what was happening with me as I was processing the events in my life.

Bass, Ellen, and Laura Davis. *The Courage to Heal, A Guide for Women Survivors of Child Sexual Abuse*. New York: Harper & Row, 1988.

Bradshaw, John. *Bradshaw on: Healing the Shame that Binds You*. Deerfield Beach, FL: Heath Communications, 1988

Bridges, William, Ph.D. *Transitions, Making Sense of Life's Changes*. Reading, MA: Addison Wesley Publishing Company, 1980.

Burns, David. *The New Mood Therapy*. New York: Avon Books, 1980

Covey, Stephen R. *The Seven Habits of Highly Effective People, Restoring the Character Ethic*. New York: Simon & Schuster, 1989.

Evans, Patricia. *Verbal Abuse Survivors Speak Out On Relationship and Recovery*. Holbrook, MA: Bob Adams, Inc., 1993.

Engle, Beverly. *The Emotionally Abused Woman, Overcoming Destructive Patterns and Reclaiming Yourself*. Los Angeles: Lowell House, 1986.

Flanagan, Beverly. *Forgiving the Unforgivable*. New York: MacMillian, 1992.

Frankl, Viktor. *The Unconscious God*. New York: Simon & Schuster, 1975.

Kasl, Charlotte Davis. *Women, Sex and Addiction, A Search for Love and Power*. New York: Ticknor & Fields, 1989.

Kolbenschlag, Madonna. *Kiss Sleeping Beauty Goodbye, Breaking the Spell of Feminine Myths and Models*. San Francisco: Harper & Row, 1979.

Kushner, Harold. *When Bad Things Happen to Good People*. New York: Schocken Books, 1981.

Levine, Stephen. *Healing into Life and Death*. New York: Doubleday, 1987.

Norwood, Robin. *Women Who Love Too Much, When You Keep Wishing and Hoping He'll Change*. Los Angeles: Jeremy Tarcher, Inc., 1985

Peck, M. Scott, M.D. *The Road Less Traveled*. New York: Simon & Schuster, 1978.

Peele, Stanton, with Archie Brodsky. *Love and Addiction*. New York: Signet, 1976.

Peele, Stanton, with Archie Brodsky. *The Truth About Addiction and Recovery, The Life Process Program for Outgrowing Destructive Habits*. New York: Simon & Schuster, 1991.

Russell, Diana E. H. *Sexual Exploitation, Rape, Child Sexual Abuse, and Workplace Harassment*. Beverly Hills, CA: Sage Publications, 1984.

Seligman, Martin E.P. *Learned Optimism, How to Change Your Mind and Life*. New York: Pocket Books, 1990.

Smedes, Lewis B. *Forgive and Forget, Healing the Hurts We Don't Deserve*. New York: Pocket Books, 1984.

Warschaw, Tessa Albert. *Rich Is Better, How Women Can Bridge the Gap Between Wanting and Having it All*. New York: Doubleday, 1985

Wheelis, Allen. *How People Change*. New York: Harper and Row, 1973.

Index

sexuality of spouse, 66-67
situational molester, 17, 21
Smedes, Lewis, 67
social services, 211
stranger danger, 16
support groups, 209, 218

theory,
    about child molesters 23-26
    about spouses, 45-46, 88
    assessing and using theory, 23-24,
        27, 45
therapist, choosing a, 216-217
thrall, 40
time to hurt, 100-102, 174

treatment,
    for molesters, 27, 29, 36-41
    for spouses, 85-86
truth, telling yourself the, 108-112
twenty twenty hindsight, 69-70

unconscious involvement, 48
unfair pain, 67

Victims, 151

Wheelis, Alan, 116
wife blaming, 46-48, 52-53, 57, 70-71

A graduate of the University of Chicago, Patricia Wiklund holds a Ph.D. in Clinical Psychology from the Fielding Institute in Santa Barbara, California. Wiklund has worked extensively with people who find themselves in situations or relationships they cannot control, helping them take charge of their lives and restore their hope in the human condition. Then it happened to her. As a practicing therapist, she was challenged to use what she knew for herself, rather than just for other people. This book is the result of her unwillingness to be victimized and to share what she experienced so others could benefit from her circumstances.